On Retreat With ...

This new series, published by Medio Media/Arthur James, responds to the spiritual needs of people living today's busy and stressed lifestyle. Each book in the series is designed to allow the reader to develop a space for silence and solitude and spiritual practice in the context of ordinary life or by taking a short period of withdrawal. The structure of the book allows a flexible time-table to be constructed which integrates periods of reading, physical practice or exercise, and meditation.

Bede Griffiths was a Benedictine monk who spent much of the latter part of his life living in India, where he founded a Christian monastery along the lines of a Hindu ashram as a place where people of all faiths could meet. Contemplation was the centre of his life. He died in 1993.

Also in the 'On Retreat With ...' Series

SELF AND ENVIRONMENT
Charles Brandt

ASPECTS OF LOVE
Laurence Freeman

AWAKENING
John Main

SILENT WISDOM, HIDDEN LIGHT
Eileen O'Hea

Among Bede Griffiths' other books are

THE GOLDEN STRING
(Harvill, 1954)

RETURN TO THE CENTRE
(Collins, 1976)

THE MARRIAGE OF EAST AND WEST
(Collins, 1982)

The 'On Retreat With ...' Series

THE MYSTERY
BEYOND

On Retreat With
Bede Griffiths

MEDIO MEDIA / ARTHUR JAMES

LONDON AND BERKHAMSTED

First published in Great Britain in 1997 by

MEDIO MEDIA LTD
in association with
ARTHUR JAMES LTD
70 Cross Oak Road
Berkhamsted
Hertfordshire HP4 3HZ

ISBN 0 85305 426 6

Typeset in Monotype Bulmer by
Strathmore Publishing Services, London N7

Printed and bound in Great Britain by
Guernsey Press Ltd, Guernsey, C.I.

Contents

Being on retreat:
how to do it yourself

Stay in your cell and your cell will teach you everything.
 – Saying of the Desert Fathers

The problems of the world arise from people's inability to
sit still in their own room.
 – Pascal, *Pensées*

Why set aside time for retreat?
Nature believes in retreats. Each day we virtually shut down our
active processes of mind and body for the retreat and renewal we
call sleep. Each year the animal and vegetable worlds go through
periods of deep rest we call hibernation. These are not escapes
from reality but ways of becoming more deeply attuned to reality,
respecting its ways and trusting the inherent wisdom of nature.

Between each breath there is a moment of cessation, of deep
stillness, which is not the stillness of inaction but the stillness of
non-action. Between periods of daily work we naturally trust the
mind and body when they tell us to rest. Between two thoughts
there is an instant of mental silence.

On the London Underground, many stations have a recorded
announcement each time the train stops, warning passengers step-
ping from the train to the platform to 'mind the gap'. Minding the
gap is what this book is about – helping you, we hope, to see and
respect the natural human need to retreat from action and speech

at set times so that we can return to speech and action refreshed, re-balanced and renewed.

The spiritual life is not a specialized part of daily life. Everything you do in the day, from washing to eating breakfast, having meetings, driving to work, solving problems, making more problems for yourself once you have solved them, watching television or deciding instead to read, going to a restaurant or a movie or going to church, *everything* you do is your spiritual life. It is only a matter of how consciously you do these ordinary things, how attentive you are to the opportunities they offer for growth, for enjoyment, and how mindfully, how selflessly, how compassionately you perform them. Yet to live life spiritually all the time everyone needs to take specific times to focus on the spiritual dimension before everything else.

'Set your mind on God's kingdom and his justice before everything else, and all the rest will come to you as well.' Jesus said this in his Sermon on the Mount (Matt. 6:33). Taking a time of retreat will help you discover what he means by 'kingdom' and 'justice'. It will teach you that the kingdom is not a place but an experience of presence. The kingdom is within us and all around us. And you will learn that justice means balance, harmony, order. We hunger for justice in all the activities and relationships of our lives.

Buddhists see the spiritual significance of daily life in terms of ordinary mindfulness: doing everything with awareness, wakefulness. Christians similarly have long worked at praying at all times, giving glory to God in everything they do, practising the presence of God. This does not mean going around muttering prayers to yourself all day. You would only be more distracted in what you are doing. Nor does it mean thinking about God all the time. That would make you a religious fanatic. Praying ceaselessly, practising the divine presence is not something extra we do but the way we do whatever we are doing. It is a way of *being* in the midst of action: of being-in-action.

Perhaps the best comparison is with a relationship with someone you love. The awareness, the mindfulness, of that love surrounds and permeates you and all your words and responses all the day. You do not have to be thinking of the person you love all the time but they are with you and their often silent presence transforms your consciousness. Yet at the end of the day, or whenever opportunity allows, you return to the full presence of that person. Being with them helps the relationship to grow and deepen, even when romance wears thin. The 'quality times' together are essential for the health and development of love.

How to set up a retreat

The 'On Retreat With ...' series has been prepared to help you to spend quality time in the most fundamental relationship of your life, your relationship with God. In the ground of this relationship are planted all your human relationships, even your relationship with yourself. Quality time with someone requires a certain degree of exclusivity – you say *no* to other invitations and pleasant opportunities in order to concentrate on your presence with one person. Other jobs and responsibilities go on hold. When you return to address them you will be refreshed, calmer, and you can see the problems that easily overwhelm you in a better perspective. Retreat is not escape. You make a retreat in order to address reality more realistically and courageously. Retreat does not solve your problems but it helps you deal with them in a more peaceful and hopeful way. This is the meaning of a retreat: we retreat in order to advance deeper into the mystery of love's reality.

This book can help you structure your time and set the tone for the period of retreat you are allowing yourself to take. As life today is very busy and as it often seems impossible to find time for silence, stillness, and non-action, we need all the help we can get in order to take the time of spiritual retreat which both spiritual and psychological health require.

Time and place: your cell

You do not need to take a great stretch of time to make a retreat. But you need to designate a certain period of time and stick to it. It could be an hour, a morning or afternoon, a day, a weekend, a week, three months. In some traditions five-year retreats are customary. Let's start with a couple of hours.

If it is a short time, a couple of hours, you will probably be at home. Or you may have found you have some free time when away on holiday or a business trip. You do not have to fill in the empty space in the agenda: keep it empty. Go into the emptiness and you will emerge refreshed, more fulfilled. Set the time realistically. Put your answer-phone on. Turn the television or radio off. If you need to tell someone not to disturb you for the next couple of hours, do so. Put your work away or walk away from it. Then make a space.

The early Christian monks who lived much in solitude each had a cell. A monastic cell is different from a prison cell: you choose to be there. It is a place of stability, of security, of focus. It does not have to be elaborate. Cells are simple places. A chair, a cushion on the floor, a corner of a room. Make it tidy and clean. Set up a symbol of the presence; this could be a candle – ancient symbol of the presence of Christ – a flower, an icon, a photo, a cross, a Bible, or a simple everyday object. There should be a sense of simplicity, not clutter – of beauty, not prettiness. Have a watch or clock with a timer device nearby (not a loud ticker or too prominently placed).

With steadiness and ease: your body

Your retreat is a homecoming, an integrating, a remembering. It is not a spacewalk or a mind trip. You cannot come home unless you come inside, so take time to consider that you are also taking time to *make friends with your body*. And remember that you are only singling out the body for the purpose of the retreat. In fact you are really one single-woven tapestry of body–mind soaked and grounded in spirit: one being, fully alive.

Single out the body, then, and learn that it is happy to carry you, support you, hug you. It rejoices to pump blood, breathe, digest, walk, and sleep. It is a wonderful, mystical, funny contraption in which we are incarnated, and have epiphanies and transfigurations, and are crucified and resurrected.

Whatever you do on this retreat, keep breathing. Breathe as you take breakfast, as you go for a solitary walk or do some housework in your cell. Breathe while you are on the toilet. Breathe during your spiritual reading and as you doze off to a peaceful sleep after your day of silence.

You already have the three things necessary with which to make friends with your body. They are breath, gravity, and ground. You have been breathing since you were born and you will keep doing so as long as you need to. So relax and let breath breathe you. It is closer to you than your thinking. The way you breathe determines how you feel (see how your breathing changes when you are angry, frightened, or peaceful). As you give your attention to your breath you become naturally heavy. That is gravity hugging you. Give to it. Let it take you to the ground which stands under you (*understands you*). The ground comes up to hold you, so relax and do nothing. In fact, un-do. Let it. You just pay attention to the breath as it breathes you in and out, in and out.

You might enjoy lying on your back before and/or after your meditation times, or after a walk. Lying on your back is an excellent way to start making friends with your body on this retreat. It helps turn off all the tapes playing in your head: tapes telling you to make a good impression on others, to be demure or macho, how to look sexy or respectable, how to dominate and be noticed. When you lie down, the three bony boxes of your body – the head, chest, and pelvis – stop chattering to each other for a while and relate directly to the ground instead. It is like turning gravity off for a moment.

Lie on your back with your knees bent so that your lower back is quite flat on the floor. Let your chin drop lightly towards your chest so that it is no longer pointing up to the ceiling. If this is difficult, put a folded blanket under your head, just an inch or so, no more. And stay, and wait in silence or listen to a taped talk on meditation or some music. If you doze off, so be it. When you do get up, first roll over gently on to your hands and knees. It is not helpful to yank the head straightaway in order to get up, because that immediately undoes all the work that breath, gravity, and ground have just accomplished in straightening you out and un-knotting you.

If you want to take this friendship with your body further, you could read *Awakening the Spine* by Vanda Scaravelli, *Yoga Over 50* by Mary Stewart (even if you are 25), and *Yoga and You* by Esther Myers. These three women are yoga teachers of great depth, humour, and insight.

Lectio: your mind and its emotions

Then, sitting comfortably, read a section of this book. Read slowly. The book will last a long time, longer probably than your body. So there is no need to speed-read or devour the book and get on to another one. Re-read what you have read. Let your mind settle on a part of the passage which speaks to you most deeply. This may be just a phrase, a word, an image, or an idea. Revolve around that for a while. You don't have to analyse it. Savour it. The early desert monks called this *lectio*, spiritual (rather than mental) reading.

After a period of *lectio*, which can be ten or fifteen minutes, transfer your attention to the symbol which is the focal point for your retreat-space. Let your attention move towards the symbol, into the presence in the symbol. Let thought relax and the mind be still. When thoughts, fantasies, fears, anxieties, restlessness surface, let them come and let them go. Say, 'I'm sorry, you'll have to come and see me later. I'm busy doing nothing at the moment.' They will get the message if you give it strongly; be ruthless with them and don't compromise.

Meditation: going deeper

This would be a good time now for your meditation. Depending on how long you have been meditating or if you are just beginning, decide how many periods of meditation you are going to have during your retreat. A minimum would be two a day. Don't overdo it, but if you are a regular meditator you can profitably put additional periods in. More is not automatically better, of course. Three would be moderate. Six periods would be fine if you were sure you were not straining yourself or getting greedy.

Sit down with your back straight, sit still, close your eyes. Take a few deep breaths and then breathe normally. Then, silently, begin to repeat your word, your mantra. A good Christian mantra is the word *maranatha*. It means, 'Come, Lord,' or, 'The Lord comes,' but do not think of its meaning as you say it. Say the word simply and listen to it as you say it. This is the journey of faith, the deep listening. Faith leads to love. You could also take the word *Jesus* or *abba* (an Aramaic word used by Jesus, meaning 'father'). Whatever word you choose, stay with the same word throughout the meditation (and from one meditation period to the next) so that it can progressively take you deeper, from mind to heart.

Do not say the word with force. You are not trying to blank out the mind. Do not fight the thoughts which will come to you from every direction. Keep returning to the mantra. Say the word from the beginning to the end of the meditation whether you are aware of feeling distracted or peaceful. As soon as you realize you have stopped saying the word, start saying it again. In time (anywhere between five minutes and twenty years) the mantra will lead you at moments into complete stillness and silence, beyond itself. But if you are conscious of being silent then you are not yet completely silent, so keep on saying the mantra until the Spirit takes over. You will find that you say the mantra more deeply, more finely, more delicately as time goes on. Time your meditation with a timer – not too alarming a sound. If you are new to meditation, begin with twenty minutes (or less if you really find twenty too long). Other-

[13]

wise thirty minutes is a good period to meditate for. If you have a gong, this will help lead into and out of the meditation peacefully.

After the meditation, come out slowly. Open your eyes. Pay attention to the symbol you have set up in front of you. This would be a good time to read some scripture. *The Burning Heart* would be a good book to use at this point – a collection of John Main's favourite Scripture passages with a short commentary by him. Again, read slowly, chewing and savouring the Word. Don't gulp it down. You could then listen to some music, do some yoga, draw, or paint.

Structuring your time of retreat

If you have to get back to work and daily life, take a few moments to appreciate the gift of present you have just enjoyed – let it go, be non-possessive. Read another section of this book, again slowly and savouring what appeals to you. Open yourself to the next thing you have to do and prepare to do it while keeping your mind and heart open to the presence you have just turned towards. Your prayerfulness continues into whatever you are now going to do. And you can share the fruits of peace and joy you have received with others, not by preaching, but in the way you relate to them. If you need to, pack up your retreat things reverently and get on with life.

If you have more time you can vary the elements of this retreat time. If you have a whole day, for example, you could schedule two, three, or four meditations. This will depend somewhat on your experience in meditation. Don't overdo it, and more does not mean better. If you are making the retreat with others, that will introduce another dimension of presence. Use this book together, reading it aloud. If you have a weekend or even longer you will need to schedule your time more carefully. Draw up a timetable but allow yourself to be flexible in keeping to it. Morning, midday, and evening are natural times for prayer – and before you go to bed. If you have a day or longer on retreat, do some manual work, even housecleaning, and get some exercise and fresh air. Walk in

[14]

the garden or a park. Take this book with you and stop and read a section during your walk.

Don't just do something, sit there!

You might find the voice of conscience attacking you during your retreat. 'You are wasting your time,' it will say, or, 'You are being selfish.' You will think of all the practical, urgent, problematic things you could do. You will get an insight into a situation and want to dash off to implement it. Watch these restless thoughts and they will die down and return less frequently. This is why you will benefit from scheduling your time. It will fool your bush mind into thinking you are doing something productive. But your heart will teach you that you are not trying to produce or achieve anything. You are being. You are drinking deep, in the desert of modern life, of the waters of divine being. Your work and the people you live with, will all benefit from this time of retreat, so you are not being selfish. A gentle discipline in ordering your time of retreat – whether an hour or a day or a weekend – will help awaken a sense of inner freedom from anxiety, obsession, and fear. Enjoy it: find joy in it.

Laurence Freeman

Non-duality

My whole life in the last few years has centred on non-duality. It has many forms, but to me more and more it is the answer to the problems of humanity and of religion today. As long as we remain in this world of dualities, of opposites, of conflict, we're always going to be divided and in conflict, and the only way to transcend all this conflict is to go beyond duality. Duality is the source of all. It is our divisions that are causing the tragedies of human existence, and only a doctrine and a way of life which takes us beyond the dualities can reconcile us and bring us the peace we are looking for. Every religion comes out of dualism – God and the world, God and man – and into non-dualism. Biblical Judaism itself is extremely dualistic, but later Jewish tradition, particularly in the cabbala, comes into pure non-dualism. In Hindusim and Buddhism, of course, this is fundamental.

In the fifth or sixth century before Christ there was a breakthrough in human consciousness. Until that time human beings had lived in the world of the senses, of the imagination – the world of gods and goddesses, the world of the mother. God is the mother goddess, and this wonderful world is a sacred world but also a world with much conflict in it and much violence and much evil. Humanity had to break through that world of magic and of the gods and goddesses and open itself to the transcendent Reality. This amazing breakthrough took place in the Upanishads. I consider that every educated person who is concerned with truth and reality today should at least be acquainted with the Upanishads. They're very easily available today so we've no excuse now for not having some knowledge of them. They start with this world of the senses, of human experience, of human suffering and so on, and they break through to the transcendent mystery, the Reality for which there is no name.

This is one of the great difficulties. As long as we can name things, they belong to our world of the reason and the senses and we feel at home; but when we touch Reality, there is no name. St Thomas Aquinas always said no one can say *quid est Deus* – what God is. The divine mystery is beyond all human name and form and thought, and I think today we must go beyond all names and forms and open our hearts and lives to this divine mystery. It *is* a mystery: you cannot name it, you cannot put it into words, but you can experience it. In the fifth and sixth centuries before Christ, the Hindus experienced that divine mystery. They called it 'Brahman'.

'Brahman' is a wonderful word. It has no exact meaning at all. It comes from the root *brh* which means to grow or to swell, and it seems probable that the sacrifice was the centre of all Hindu worship. You built a fire and you offered everything in the fire and the fire took it up to heaven. You offered all that you had and the god of fire, who was a messenger of the gods, carried your gifts up to heaven. As the priest was offering the sacrifice, this word would rise up in him, and he would say 'Brahman'.

The power in the sacrifice is the power in the whole universe, because in ancient thinking the whole world is based on sacrifice. To sacrifice is to make a thing sacred – and we've lost the sacred, you know. In England today, there's hardly anything sacred. There are sacred spots, but for the ordinary person the sacred no longer exists. Yet the ancient world related this world of time, space, and matter as we know it to the transcendent Reality. To make a thing sacred is to open it to the divine, to the transcendent, and everything ought to be made sacred in that way. In India today it is still very wonderful: eating and drinking and bathing, for example, are all sacred actions.

The traditional Hindu practice, which we do not always follow, is to have a banana leaf and put your rice and your food on the banana leaf, then take some water and sprinkle it round the leaf and make a sacred space. You keep out all the contrary forces. Water purifies that space and then you offer that food to the divine, and the divine power consumes it in your stomach. The chant from the Bhagavad Gita is used: 'I, the Lord seated in the body, become the power of life and consume the four kinds of food.' You offer it in the fire of your belly to the divine. It is accepted and surrendered, so your food becomes sacred and is a means of union with God.

So the ancient tradition saw the world as essentially sacred; it had to be consecrated to God, and so everything in this world was related to the transcendent Reality. Then in the fifth and sixth centuries before Christ they got beyond the gods and the goddesses and the spirits and all these outer forms, and discovered the nameless, formless Reality which they called 'Brahman' or *atman* or the Buddha. Buddhism has a wonderful message for everybody: the Buddha broke through all this world of the senses, all the passions and all the desires, and let everything go. He reached a sort of total annihilation; and when he had annihilated the world he discovered *nirvana*, the Reality behind the world, behind everything, and that is pure joy.

What joy it is to have found *nirvana* – to have found the way and be full of joy. We must get beyond the world of the senses, time and space, and the whole of our scientific world, and realize the reality which is reflected in the scientific world but infinitely transcends it. We must be able to go beyond all the time.

Now this brings me to a real problem. In India, they tend to say that Brahman is real but the world is unreal – the world is *maya*, an illusion. Everything, the table and the chair, you and I and God, any form of God – all this is illusion. But that kind of negative approach is very harmful. I think it is very unsound, actually: friends who have studied Shankara in depth tell me it is not Shankara's conception of *adwita*. For Shankara, the world of our senses, the whole physical universe, has no reality in itself – but it has reality

in relation to the supreme, to Brahman. It is in that, and not in ourselves, that we have reality, truth, joy, and fulfilment. So Shankara
was really saying this world has a purely relative reality.

Interestingly, this is exactly the teaching of St Thomas Aquinas.
Sarah Grant, a Sacred Heart sister in Poona, tells me that
Shankara's teaching, properly understood, is identical with that of
St Thomas Aquinas: that the world has no existence in itself at all,
but has existence in relation to God, to the Ultimate.

How can we learn to accept this world? We don't have to deny
the world, our family, our friends, our homes, our gardens, and our
work. All this is real, but its reality is not in itself. The idolatry
which we all commit is thinking this is the real: I think that this
table is real in itself, and I just go on examining the table; but the
table has no reality in itself. Its reality is only in and through and
from Brahman, from *the* reality, the one reality manifested in all
these different forms. The forms keep coming and going and
changing, but the one reality, the one word, the one truth is manifested in all these forms.

That was the breakthrough made by the Upanishads and the
Buddha; and although the breakthrough came in India, it was for all
humanity. These things don't happen twice. We inherit the message
of the Buddha and the Upanishads, and today it is wonderful to see
how it is spreading all over Europe and America. People are dis-
covering this wisdom of the East – the Upanishads, the Bhagavad
Gita, the Dhammapada, and still more perhaps the Mahayana.

There is always the danger of thinking that the created world, even
if it is not an absolute illusion, is unimportant. But the genuine
adwita, as developed in Mahayana Buddhism and particularly in
Tibet, recognizes that *samsara* (the world of change and becoming,
of life and death as we know it) is the same as *nirvana* (the end of all
suffering and death and change). This is a wonderful insight, but you
cannot get this insight as long as you remain on the merely rational
level. The rational, logical mind is created to divide, to analyse, to
break things up.

It is wonderful what we have done. The Greek philosophers started dividing the world up, and Western science carried it to the limit, breaking it up into more and more pieces. Everything in this world was understood as solid, separate objects moving in space and time – Newton's system, with the earth and the planets moving round the sun. This wonderful construction lasted for two hundred years or more. The idea was to try to break matter down into smaller and smaller particles until they reached the atom – the word comes from the Greek adjective *atomos*, meaning 'that which cannot be cut or divided'. Atoms, they thought, were the building blocks of the universe. Since atoms obeyed mathematical laws, people only had to understand the mathematical laws of atoms and they would understand the universe.

And then the breakthrough came with Einstein's great discovery of quantum physics in the 1920s – you see, it is only seventy years old. They found they could split the atom, and when they split the atom they got a lot of other particles – electrons, neutrons, and all the rest. Then the critical moment came in the 1920s when they realized these particles also were not ultimate. It was impossible to distinguish between particles and waves.

This was shattering: the whole vision of the universe was collapsing. All these solid bodies had suddenly disappeared and there were nothing but waves of energy. Today in science they say the universe is a field of energies working at different frequencies, and we're all part of this field of energies. We are all worked into it as part of our very being and in that world of the energies we construct these forms and figures and these solid bodies and all the rest. We project this universe around us.

The great authority on this is David Bohm, who wrote *Wholeness and the Implicate Order*. He is a very great scientist apparently, a disciple of Einstein, but at the same time he is a very genuine philosopher and very interestingly he is one of the few scientists who has learnt to meditate. In meditation you have to go beyond your rational mind and all these divisions of the sense world and discover the non-dual reality, which is beyond it all. I believe it is only in meditation that we can reach that reality, because in meditation we first of all try to harmonize the body and the senses. You don't try to suppress the body, but you try to bring it into a calm and quiet state, and then you try to harmonize the mind, stopping all mental activity, letting it subside, letting it become calm and quiet. When the body and the mind are under control, calm and quiet, this non-dual awareness awakens, beyond your thoughts, feelings, and desires.

Non-duality is neither one nor two. It does not mean that the world is simply one and there is no difference (or at least, somebody may have held that but that is not the truth). Nor does it mean that God and the world are two separate entities, God there and the world here. That is an illusion – a useful illusion, for we have to think like that, but when we think seriously we know that God and the world are not two. The world has a purely relative being. As I say, St Thomas Aquinas was as clear about this as Shankara or any other oriental philosopher. The world has no reality except in relation to Brahman, to the supreme.

I do not know any science apart from what I read in popular books such as Fritjof Capra's *The Tao of Physics*, which is a wonderful book for the non-scientist. It describes this universe as a complex web of interdependent relationships. We are all parts of this interrelated universe. The whole is in every part, and nothing happens in any part of the universe which does not affect the whole. The galaxy is an interrelated whole. This is a marvellous vision of each one of us as a physical body that is related to every other physical being in the universe.

Who am I? I'm this being, sitting here talking to you, thinking, writing, and so on – but that is my ego. There is a conscious self. I have conscious feelings and desires; I have conscious thoughts, will, and so on, which make up my conscious self. We cannot live without this conscious self, but it is a terribly limited thing, this separate self. The cause of all our conflicts is that each of us is a separate self. From childhood we grow up with the idea that we are separate selves, but that is an illusion. We are not separate selves. Depth psychology has opened us up to the understanding that this conscious ego is just a small portion of our real being; beyond the conscious ego is the vast depth of the unconscious, what Jung called the collective unconscious. If I go beyond and behind my ego consciousness, I discover a whole emotional world in my links with other people: my relation with my mother and my family, blood relationships, all these things are to be found in the unconscious. And beyond that, beyond my relations with human beings, I can discover my relation to the universe. All of us, deep in our unconscious, are linked to the original explosion of matter. Fifteen thousand million years ago this matter exploded, and that matter is in us.

Time and space are all aspects of this total reality which is in our unconscious. We think of it in terms of time and space, making all these theories about it, but we are all part of this cosmic whole. That, of course, if why ecology is becoming such a vital subject today. We lost part of that: we thought we could do what we liked with the world around us; we have been abusing it and polluting it and destroying it, and now it is beginning to destroy us. Actually, we do not know what is going to happen to the universe around us; that is the effect of this conscious mind being unaware of its links with the whole of matter, the whole of life, the whole of the animal world, and the whole of the human world. We are all parts of this cosmic whole.

A new vision is now dawning. Physical scientists are opening up to the world as a field of energies. David Bohm uses the analogy of a hologram: if you make a hologram portrait of somebody, and look at it under a laser beam or some strong light source, the three-dimensional portrait is revealed. Interestingly, every part of the photo shows the whole face. So the idea has grown up that we are all part of this universe of vibrating energies and, within that as it were, as these three-dimensional wholes which we observe.

Around us we see the world with all that is in it, but it is all contained within the cosmic whole; the trees, the animals, and so on are interrelated, interdependent aspects of the one cosmic whole.

This vision which is gradually dawning today is very exciting. It changes one's whole understanding of life – and the important thing is that this is bringing us back to the understanding of the universe in the fifth and sixth centuries before Christ, as developed in the Hindu, Buddhist, Taoist, and all oriental doctrine. Western scientists, in particular, when they study matter, are used to analysing it and observing all its different degrees, but they are coming to discover that all matter is simply this field of energies.

Eastern philosophers, by contrast, observed the mind. The subtlety of observation of the processes of the mind is incredible. They sat in meditation and they watched their thoughts – and it's a very good exercise still. By watching their thoughts like that, they discovered how the mind works; they discovered that these concepts of the mind, by which we label people and things and so on, and divide the world, are all limiting concepts. They are all contained within a deeper vision, a wholeness which transcends all these limiting thoughts. Shankara was the great master for Hinduism; in Buddhism it was Nagarjula. I have not studied him in depth at all but he was a Brahman philosopher of the second century AD and the founder of the Madhyamika School of Mahayana Buddhism, teaching particularly in Tibet. He has exactly the same view. He analysed the whole process of conceptual thought and realized that the conceptual mind cannot grasp reality. No science and no philosophy grasps reality. We form conceptual structures by which we organize the world around us, but the reality is always beyond our structures, our concepts, our systems, our theories. They are all useful in pointing towards it, but none of them is even remotely adequate. And so Nagarjuna said that beyond the discursive mind with all its concepts and judgments is *prajhe* – the root of the word is the same as the English 'know' or German 'können'. *Prajhe* is knowledge which goes beyond all the multiplicity of the world and of thoughts, and inside into *the* reality.

At that period, they gained an insight into reality. The Buddha called it *nirvana* – 'void', 'emptiness'. Ultimately, all these differences which we see around us have no reality in themselves; they are all contained within the void, this emptiness, which is also fullness. It is a paradox, of course, that the emptiness is the fullness; so, as we go beyond our rational mind and our senses and so on, we discover wholeness. It is a mystical experience. That is why it is difficult. Today, people are afraid of mysticism: it will lead you don't know where. And of course, it is important when we go beyond the rational mind that we do not deny it in any way. As you transcend any level of consciousness you have to integrate it in the higher. Your consciousness observes all the sensory phenomena around you, and as your rational mind develops you do not deny them, but you integrate them. When you attain this higher level of consciousness to the deeper wisdom, you integrate mental consciousness and scientific concepts in the higher wisdom.

We might go mad if we lost our scientific and rational knowledge, but we are not to lose it but rather to integrate it in the higher knowledge. This is the challenge facing us all today. We cannot remain on this level of rational, conceptual, analytical knowledge. It divides everything, it divides up the universe, it divides up human beings, it divides religions, it divides philosophy; it is called 'the learned knife' because it cuts everything to pieces. That is why we quarrel and fight all the time over our religions and our philosophies. When we go beyond the rational mind, however, and open ourselves to this transcendent mystery, we are set free from these limitations, and we discover the unity behind it all. You cannot speak of it properly – there is no word that can express it – but you can experience it, and that is the challenge today.

That is why many of us practise meditation. It is a practical method of going beyond your senses, beyond your mind, and opening yourself to this transcendent mystery – call it God, or truth, or love, or whatever word you like. No word can describe it, but it opens you up to a depth of meaning and reality which transforms your life and can transform the life of the world. I am fully convinced that as long as we remain in our present consciousness – the rational, scientific, divisive consciousness which involves science and philosophy and politics and religion – as long as we remain on that level, we are going to quarrel and fight one another. Only when we transcend that dualism of the mind and open ourselves up to the non-dual reality, the mysterious truth which is there all the time, only then are we free from the conflict and tragedy of the world. This is an urgent call to all of us to go beyond this divisive mind. Meditation is important as one of the principal means of going beyond.

There are other ways. The unselfish way is one way of going beyond your ego, beyond all the dualisms and opening yourselves up. But meditation is perhaps the most direct means, so I feel we must take the step now at the end of the second millennium. We have to take this step forward, for humanity as a whole has got to transcend this divisive, rational, scientific, conceptual mind without denying its values; it must open up to the non-dual reality which is in every religion.

I am writing a book, *The Universal Wisdom,** giving extracts from all the seven main religions of the world. I show how each one begins with dualism and slowly, at various stages, transcends the dualism and reaches the non-dual mystery. The biggest problem is with Judaism, Christianity and Islam; they are all very dualistic religions. God and the world are two, they are separate; and man and woman are separate; and men are separate from one another. Everything is separate and divided.

But in the Bible itself there is continuous movement to go beyond all this, to return to paradise. Paradise was before all this

---

* *Universal Wisdom: A Journey Through the Sacred Wisdom of the World*, (Fount, London), 1994.

division took place, and is also the idea of the New Covenant when the law will be written in the heart. This is to be found all through the Old Testament: think of the new creation in Isaiah, which goes beyond the present creation, time and space, and so on. The movement in the Bible is through the dualities to the non-duality.

I am convinced that Jesus was taking the church and humanity beyond the dualities of the Jewish tradition into this non-dual mystery. It is expressed in St John's Gospel in the most powerful way where he says Jesus prays to God 'that they may be one, as we are one; I in them and thou in me, may they be perfectly one' (John 17:22-23). Jesus has this non-dual relationship to the Father. He is not the Father – Jesus is not God in that sense. I think it is very dangerous to call him God. Jesus has this unique relationship to the Father: he is in the Father, the Father is in him, he who sees him sees the Father, he has the love of the Father, the knowledge – it is all a non- dual relationship. They are not two and they are not one, and that is the relationship of love. The outward reality is love, and love is non-dual. When you love somebody completely you give yourself totally to them; they give themselves to you. You become totally one and yet you are two; you are not two and yet you are not simply one. You do not lose yourself in love, you find yourself. So Jesus and the Father have this total oneness and yet distinction. The Hindu says, 'I am Brahman.' It is a wonderful insight, but the danger is that he identifies with Brahman, and his individual self disappears, whereas in love you do not disappear, you surrender yourself totally, you go beyond your ego, your limited self, and you find your real self in God, in Brahman.

Jesus finds himself in the Father and he calls us to share in that non-dual relationship with the Father, 'that they may be one, as we are one; I in them and thou in me'. That is Christian non-dualism. From that point it developed through the Christian mystics.

Meister Eckhart is becoming recognized more and more as the great spiritual master of the Middle Ages, and he brought Christianity to pure non-dualism. It is a wonderful achievement, but in every religion it is the same. In Hinduism and in Mayahana Buddhism, as I say, it is equally clear. In Taoism it is beautiful; the *I Ching* has the same doctrine, and is a wonderful book. Islam is a very dualistic religion, all about God and judgment and condemnation, but the Sufi mystics took the Qur'an beyond all this dualism into pure non-dualism. There is a great Sufi mystic, Ibn al-'Arabi, whose *Bezels of Wisdom* has been translated and edited by a very wonderful English scholar, R. W. J. Austin, and published in the Classics of Western Spirituality series. It is a wonderful book. Austin has translated it, commented and explained the whole doctrine. Ibn al-'Arabi takes the God – Allah – of the Qur'an beyond the limits of the personal God. The great problem is that for the Semitic people God is a person and you must worship that person. He is Yahweh, there is no other name for God but Yahweh; or he is Allah, there is no other name but Allah. But Ibn al-'Arabi says that, beyond what he calls the God created in belief, beyond Allah, is *al haqq*, the reality, and so his whole teaching focusses on the reality.

Thus each religion goes beyond the personal God which is a projection. All our personal Gods are projections of our minds, and this personal form which we project is useful and indeed necessary at a certain stage. But we have to go beyond the personal form to the formless One in each religion. Eckhart makes the distinction between God and the Godhead. God is the personal God you worship and pray to, but the Godhead is that from which the God as you conceive it comes. It is the transcendent mystery beyond name and form; and so it is also for Ibn al-'Arabi.

I have not studied Judaism much, but in the fourteenth century, particularly in Spain, they reached the same point. They called the Supreme Reality *En Sof*, the Infinite. The one infinite, eternal reality is beyond Yahweh and all the personal God and all the conflicts which that creates.

So in each tradition we are being carried beyond duality to the non-dual mystery, and I think this is the challenge for all of us today. We cannot stay with these limited human concepts of God and religion as Christians and Jews and Muslims have them. They have their place, of course; you always integrate the other levels of consciousness, you do not deny them. But you have to go beyond and realize the transcendent mystery to which all concepts, images, thoughts, and desires point – to this Infinite Mystery beyond. This is what I feel we are challenged to do at the end of this millennium. The human race must go beyond these dualities; otherwise we are going to destroy one another. We have been doing it in one war after another, and people are still doing it in so many places. And look at our religions – they are all quarrelling, Jews and Christians and Muslims and so on. We will always quarrel, but beyond all the dualisms – of religion and names and forms and concepts and judgments and images – beyond all these is the non-dual mystery which embraces all and transcends all; and that is the object of our human quest.

Questions

What you have been saying does not mean syncretism, does it? By acknowledging the One and going to the Source then one respects the differences.

Syncretism is mixing: you take a bit of Hinduism, a bit of Buddhism, a bit of Christianity, and you put them together. That is a deception. You must respect each tradition as having its own unique value and insight. Christian, Hindu, Buddhist, Muslim, whatever you like, each has a unique value, a unique insight, and we respect these values and insights. We realize that they are all limited, historically and socially, and linguistically conditioned, but beyond all the divisions and distinctions is the non-dual mystery from which they all come. You can be fully Christian and believe in Christ and God the Father and all the rest and keep your

Christian faith, but the revelation is limited historically in time and space. You must respect the other revelations of Hinduism, Buddhism, and so on. We must learn to respect the different modes in which the Divine Mystery has revealed itself from the beginning. I always like to quote the Australian aborigines: they have been in Australia for 40,000 years, and they have a wonderful religion. It has nothing to do with Christianity, but God was there and he was teaching them to know him in a different way for 40,000 years. So there is a plan in human history. It is the same with the American Indians, or native Americans as they call them. They have a wonderful religion which is always a cosmic religion: God is manifested in creation in the earth, in the water, in the animals, in the flowers, in the trees, in the world around them. So each religion has its own values and insights. We have to respect each and yet remain faithful to our own religious tradition with its own unique insight and value. That is how I would put it.

You have said very clearly how so many of the great religions have become non-dual and evolved. The last thing I want to suggest that science could ever become a religion, but it is an exciting time in science at the moment as well. Do you think science has the capacity to become non-dual or is it essentially couched in dualistic language with no escape?

No, I think definitely in David Bohm it has reached that point already. It is amazing, and there are other scientists moving in the same direction. It is extraordinary, nobody would have dreamed it twenty, thirty, or forty years ago, but now the leading scientists are able to say that this universe really is a whole; all the distinctions we make are necessary for our limited mind and instruments and services, but they are all aspects of a transcendent whole. That is David Bohm's understanding, so really science and religion have settled their problems.

You have said that all the wrongs of humanity lie in ignorance of this one reality. Can you say something about ignorance? Why is it so pervasive?

I think it is really due to the limited condition of the human being. After all, we are all born into this world with these physical limitations, psychological limitations, the limitations of our family, and so on. We are all born into this world with limited intelligence and limited experience, but we are born to transcend it. We have to go through the limitations; we have to increase. A child has to acquire a self and some knowledge of science and so on, and then go beyond. Ignorance is simply a stage in knowledge really. It is a stage through which we have to pass to ever greater knowledge; and the final knowledge is the knowledge of non-duality.

You said we have to transcend dualism to become free, and that meditation and unselfish love are two of the ways. But you said there were other ways. What are they?

I think a sculptor or artist who dedicates himself to his work – or even anybody else who really gives himself to work unselfishly – can get beyond the dualism. I think probably many very simple people do. Even the mother of a family, simply doing the work of bringing up the children, is getting beyond the ego. Anything that makes you really unselfish, giving yourself, is a way to non-duality, to fulfilment. And then, of course, there is devotional love, and I think one can include in that human love. I honestly believe that human love, sexual love, can be a means of opening to the divine. You see the male and the female are made for one another and it is not merely a physical relationship, an animal relationship. It is a relationship of the integral human being. We are all both male and female, and when the man and the woman unite the total human being comes, and when you reach your total humanity you open up to God, you find that God is in your total oneness, so I think that is a way to God. It is a very dangerous way perhaps – you get lost in it easily – but I think it can be a way for people. But of course, more obviously, bhakti is devotion to God, to the saints, to the angels, to the gods; and all these forms of devotion are tremendous. We should not despise the devotion to the gods in Hinduism, for instance. Hindus have all sorts of local gods. A god is a projection of your unconscious, an archetype, and it focusses your energies, your love, on some particular form of the Absolute, and so you give yourself with all your might to that form and through that you can come to the Absolute. You can always go through the form to the Formless One, so *bhakti* in all its forms can be a means. Wisdom (*jnana*) is the ideal way really, and meditation is the way of *jnana*; but there are probably other ways as well.

You have given a full description of the mind, but where is the soul?

I make a distinction between the soul and the spirit. This is very important. It comes in St Paul: body (*soma*), soul (*psuche*), and spirit (*pneuma*). The soul is the psyche and the spirit is the *pneuma* or the *atman*; unfortunately we confuse the two. The early Fathers had this body, soul, and spirit, but Aristotle's psychology took over and most Christians think of the human being as a body/soul. Now the problem with that is that you here are body/soul and God is somewhere out there, separate, distinct. But the spirit is the point where the human and the divine meet, in the depth of your being. Beyond your psyche with all its limitations is your *pneuma* where the spirit of man meets the Spirit of God and that is where non-duality comes in. So the spirit is beyond the psyche and the fall of man is the fall from the spirit into the psyche, into the ego. Instead of being in your spirit, united with God, drawing everything into the life of the spirit into God, you fall into your psyche, your ego, and from this come all our divisions. That is our human state, and we are being called to come out of the psyche with its limitations, through the spirit into the divine, into the fullness of life as it's called.

Where does the animal kingdom fit in to your non-dual picture?

I think the spirit integrates the whole creation. We make these distinctions, the physical universe and then the animal and then the human, but actually the whole creation, physical, psychological, is contained within the fullness of the spirit. It is our divisive mind which makes up all these divisions between physical and psychological and so on, but when we transcend that we realize we do not lose the physical universe and the whole psychological universe. They are there but their limitations and divisions are transcended, they are realized in their fullness. An example occurs to me. They say Mozart could conceive a whole symphony in a single flash of light. The whole symphony would be present to him. Well that is non-dual. He could work it out later, all the notes of everything in detail but it was all there. So we have everything worked out in detail but when you get beyond, to the whole, it is to perceive the whole reality in its oneness; and that is the goal. I think that is heaven. When you reach that, you see the whole universe and the whole creation in its oneness in God, totally one. All the differences will be there but limited; the divisions will be transcended.

Could you tell us please about the Holy Trinity?

Oh yes, it's a wonderful subject. I am very much against this monad, this monotheism. The one God up there is a great obstacle to many Christians and Jews and others today, though thinking of a God up there is a necessary stage. All the critics say today that Jesus' whole life was based on his experience as God as Father.

[33]

Abba is Aramaic for 'father', and Jesus saw his whole life in terms of intimate relationship to the Father, to God. If you read St John's Gospel in particular, but all through the New Testament, you see this marvellous intimacy. Jesus is one with the Father and yet he is not the Father, and that is a relationship with love. The Father is the source of all, the origin, the one, and from the source of all comes this expression of his being. A Word expresses the being and the Word of God is the expression of being, of truth, of reality; all is contained in that Word, and so when the source, the Father, begets himself, manifests himself, in the Son it makes this bond of love. The Holy Spririt is the love which flows between the Father and the Son. John Main had a beautiful expression, that in meditation we seek to enter into the consciousness of Christ and the consciousness of Christ is the stream of love which flows between the Father and the Son and is the Holy Spirit; and that is the Trinity. It's wonderful. The ultimate reality is not a monad, a single person up there; it is a communion of love, and we are all being called to participate in that communion of interpersonal love. That is the end of human existence, and Jesus realized in his person the communion with the Father and the Spirit. I think there's a fullness in this Christian Trinity which you don't find elsewhere, but there are indications everywhere of it.

Did you say God is an archetype?

No, I certainly didn't. Jung would say God was an archetype. I don't think I would. You see the archetypes, I would say images, are in the unconscious. We project these images of God and spirits and angels and gods and so on, and they are very real and meaningful. It all depends what you mean. If you mean the mere personal God, then he can be an archetype, but God himself as the reality, the truth, is beyond all the archetypes, beyond all images. We must always go beyond any image, any concept of God to the reality beyond it; and of course the Trinity is as near as we can get to the truth beyond the mere personal God. The personal God is a big problem I think for many people today.

In your book, A New Vision of Reality,* *you talk about how human consciousness has gone through various stages. I found it very comforting that you say that each stage that is transcended is not thrown out. You can take it on as a small part of this consciousness. But is this the universe coming to see the creator?*

Exactly, I think so. You see the universe is becoming conscious in us. Consciousness was latent in the universe at that explosion of matter. How can you explain the extraordinary mathematical order of the universe? There must be some intelligence in that matter from the beginning, and that intelligence begins to become conscious in us, and as we grow in consciousness we are carried by that intelligence to the supreme intelligence, the supreme consciousness, so the whole universe is becoming conscious through humanity and is opening itself to the full consciousness of the supreme.

You said that there was a unique revelation within every religion. Why are you a Catholic rather than anything else?

I think we begin with the limitations of our religion. I was an Anglican to begin with and I was converted to Catholicism – it was all part of my growth. A Hindu is a Hindu because he is brought up in Hinduism, and a Buddhist is a Buddhist, because he is brought up in that, but I think each of us has to grow, and today we

---

* *A New Vision of Reality: Western Science, Eastern Mysticism and Christian Faith*, (Fount, London), 1992.

cannot remain in these compartments. We begin to discover the other religious traditions. And you see my experience (and there are many others like it) has been that the more I open myself to the values and insights of the Hindu and Buddhist and Sufi and other traditions, the more my understanding of the Christian revelation grows. It expands and enriches and it becomes wonderful; so that confirms me in my faith. I suppose if it had gone differently and if I had found that Hinduism gave me something that Christianity could not, I might have changed. I don't know. But I have always found an enrichment and a growth and a process of fulfilment, and I think each one must follow his own light, whether he is a Hindu or a Buddhist – or an atheist for that matter. An atheist has his own understanding of truth and justice very often. You must follow the light and keep open to wherever the light leads you. You see in different religions, or philosophies; and the one demand on all of us is to be true to our inner self. You see the inner light within, and therefore you are led to your goal, whatever it may be. Mine has kept me in the church.

I have a tendency to dabble with different religions. Is it necessary to follow a single path?

Yes, this is very important. I think there is a stage when one can dabble with different religions, but definitely you have to reach a point where you begin to discern a deeper truth behind all the differences. Unless you discern that deeper reality, that deeper truth, you are not on the right track and you can go on dabbling to the end of your life and get nowhere. I think that at a certain stage it can be very helpful to explore different religions, but you must get beyond that stage and discover your own deep self and how to integrate the different aspects into your reality, your truths. We all have a truth within us, a deep reality, and that is what we have to follow.

You have spoken about pain and suffering, and you give wonderful examples of how beyond pain and suffering there is an 'ocean of love'. I wonder if you would say something about that, because people find the problems of the world today very difficult to understand.

I had a stroke in 1989. I was sitting meditating in the morning and something hit me on the head, like a sledge hammer, I was absolutely knocked out. I very nearly died – I thought I was going to die – and apparently I did not speak for a week; but as I came round it was extraordinary. It had knocked down the sort of divisive, scientific, rational mind and the deeper mind began to emerge. But through this sort of death I came to the greater reality. Unless something breaks down your normal, conventional world you cannot get beyond it; that is why sickness, pain, and loss have positive value if you learn to accept them. I am told that when people are dying they resent it very much at first; they fight against it and get angry; but the moment they learn to accept it, to see this as the will of God, they can be totally transformed. They let themselves go, and something deeper takes over and transforms them. The whole secret is to let go of the ego, and anything that knocks the ego down will save you. Even the most painful loss, such as the loss of a wife or a child in an accident, is a way in which you can open yourself to the Divine, to the Truth.

I think you said that you thought it was the female aspect that hit you on the side of the head?

It's a very interesting experience. I think I was male dominated to a great extent, and when I was coming round after this thing, a week or so afterwards, I thought I was going to die; when that didn't happen I felt a bit at a loss, and something said to me, 'Surrender to the mother.' It came out of the blue, and I surrendered and a sort of wave of love came over me. It was extraordinary. I called out to somebody, 'I'm being overwhelmed by love.' I think the feminine, which I had probably suppressed, was opened up and was just surging up in me and invading. It is a good example of how suppressed feelings prevent your growth; if something can break through your outer shell, then you become whole again. The male and the female have to unite in every person. Marriage is only a way. Union has to be within each person. The marriage has to take place and that's the real goal, then you become whole.

I feel a sort of transcendent bliss in this hall tonight, but when we leave we shall encounter all the razzmatazz of election night. How do we carry this bliss of non-dualism into life?

I think really through meditation. If you set apart a time every day, let it all go, the election or whatever it may be. Simply be in the Presence – it renews you day by day. You may find you are very distracted and cannot get rid of it all, but if you persevere I think you will recover the bliss. It is there all the time, and if you can only calm yourself sufficiently and let go, the bliss will return to you.

The inner journey

I would like to consider meditation as a way of transcending differences. The great problem of our world is that we are all divided – particularly the religious world – and these divisions are terrible. I was speaking to a friend from Northern Ireland who has been working there with Catholics and Protestants. She says it is almost terrifying. Everybody thinks they are right. The Catholics are convinced that the Catholic church is the only true church, that you must belong to the Catholic church. For the Protestants, popery is sinful, idolatry; you must have nothing to do with it.

So we divide ourselves. All the Christian churches are divided against one another and all of them think they are right. The Roman church is absolutely convinced it is the one, true church. The Orthodox are equally convinced that they are the one true church and in Mount Athos they will not receive with Catholics at communion. And, of course, Protestants say that Orthodox and Catholics are idolators and superstitious, and for the evangelical Protestant biblical religion is the one true religion. So we are all equally convinced. Then, of course, you come to the Muslims. They are absolutely convinced that Muhammad was the prophet of God, that the Qur'an was dictated by the Archangel Gabriel to Muhammad, and that its every word is the word of God. They say Jews and Christians also are people of the book, with their prophets and so on; that Jesus was a great prophet, but that Christians have corrupted the Scriptures. They say the Qur'an says it is impossible for God to have a son, but the Christians pretend that God had a son. So Islam is is the one true religion and Christianity and all other religions are false.

[39]

The Hindus and Buddhists are different in a way. They say it is all true. They definitely do not deny any, but then they do not make any distinctions really. For a Hindu, it does not really matter if you are a Christian or a Jew or a Muslim – it's all the same.

So we are all divided and we have to find some way in which we can go beyond these divisions which arise as soon as we begin to talk. When you begin to think and to talk you have to form images and concepts and judgments; you make a system, and that is where the divisions begin. People need to get beyond the images, beyond the concepts, beyond the doctrines to the source; and the source of all religion is not in doctrines or in rituals or in any category at all. It is the transcendent mystery. Karl Rahner, who was the great theologian of our century, again and again particularly towards the end of his life was insisting that all this talk about God is inadequate. Nothing you can say about God is remotely adequate. God is infinite, transcendent mystery which we have to adore and worship and to love, but it is beyond every image and thought we could conceive, and meditation is how we get beyond.

In meditation, as many of you know, we have to begin with the body. We are human beings, and the soul and the mind cannot act without the body. If we neglect the body, we neglect an essential aspect of our personality, of our being; and, of course, in the West we tend to neglect the body. We feel that in prayer the body does not matter very much. But in the East, from the earliest times, *hatha yoga* begins with control of the body, and I think we all have to learn to relax the body. Nearly everybody, especially here in the West, is tense, and the mind affects the body. People get arthritis and so on, all because the mind is so constricted that it causes problems in the body. So we have to begin with the body, and relax the muscles. We have to become conscious of the body and to harmonize. They say yoga is harmonizing the body, and many do it consciously. If you relax and harmonize the eyes and the nose, the mouth, the throat, the chest, the legs, the feet, the whole body has to be relaxed and surrendered to God. Your body is a temple of the

Holy Spirit, St Paul said, and we have to surrender the body to God. It is very important. We must be conscious of the body.

Then the next thing is the breathing. They say the link between the body and the mind is the breath. If your mind is agitated your breath gets agitated, and if your mind is calm the breath is calm. If you calm your breathing, you can calm your mind. So we breathe quietly, deeply, from the abdomen, the most important part of the body, the centre of all the energy. I am told that two thirds of the blood in the body is all centred in the abdomen, so it is a real physical centre. When we breathe we should breathe from the belly, from the depths, and let it rise up and come down. So the whole body is in rhythm, in harmony, and we have to be in harmony with the environment. We all live in this world where we are all interrelated with the air around us, with the sun, and with all the forces of nature; we have to be in harmony with the universe around us, and this quiet, relaxed sitting and breathing is how we harmonize our whole being with the universe. It is all very important, and we often neglect this aspect in prayer. So we begin with the body and with the breath; and then, of course, we come to the mind, which is where all the real problems begin.

For us in the West it is the great problem. We train the mind from the earliest ages possible. I was lucky – I think now they start even earlier – but I began to learn French when I was four, and Latin when I was seven, and Greek when I was nine, and I went on learning until I was about twenty-one, studying, using the mind all the time. We are all trained like that to use our minds, and after a time you cannot control the mind. So we have to learn how to relax the mind, and for most people that is the most difficult problem.

How can you calm the mind? The *Yoga Sutra* of Patanjali is the classical system of Yoga. It begins with the cessation of the movements of the mind, and when we enter into meditation we must learn to stop the mind, to relax the body and the breathing. You cannot actually stop the mind, but you can allow it to become still. There are two main methods. The Buddhists generally use simply the breathing. You observe your breathing, observe your sensations. It is one of the most popular methods of meditation.

There is a wonderful leader in India, Goenka. He is a Burmese who has a centre near Poona where he gives meditation courses year after year. Hundreds of people of all walks of life go, and it is very strict. You are not normally allowed to read or to write or to smoke, or to go out at any time. For at least ten hours a day you have to meditate. It is done very carefully, with some periods of relaxation and so on, but everybody says it is very difficult at first; but they all say it is wonderful. I know many priests and sisters and others have found it extremely helpful; you simply observe your breathing and then you observe the sensations in your head and eyes and nose. You go through your whole body observing your sensations, and you are learning to detach yourself from the body. You do not reject it, of course, you are observing and accepting it, but you are detached from it. This detachment is really the great secret.

The other thing is to allow the thoughts to come and go and to observe your thoughts. Unfortunately in our Christian tradition we believe that some thoughts are good and some thoughts are bad and you must reject bad thoughts, since they are sinful. I think that is very harmful. You have to learn to observe your thoughts, all your bad thoughts, your sexual thoughts and images and things that come up. It is no good just pushing them down: they come back worse and worse. The more you suppress, the more they come back in a negative way, but when you learn to observe them in a detached way, not indulging them and not suppressing them but quietly observing them, then you get a detached attitude to yourself. You learn to observe yourself, what you are doing all the time. Mostly we are not conscious of what we are doing; we are just reacting to people and things. But when we learn to detach and to observe we become aware of ourselves. For the Buddhist this awareness, this watchfulness, is the key thing, and I think we all need to learn it. As Christians we all need to learn these different methods of meditation – yoga – which have been practised in the East for thousands of years. They have been tried out by masters again and again and they are authentic ways of meditation and self-discipline.

So we try to observe the breathing, observe the sensations, and observe the thoughts. For most of us Christians, the simplest way of gaining this control over the mind is the use of a mantra.

Before John Main became a monk, he was a lawyer in Malaya, where he met a Hindu swami who made a tremendous impression on him. From this swami he learned to pray with the mantra, a sacred word you repeat, and this took hold of him and he found an answer to his need. He then joined the monastery at Ealing and they told him, 'That's all pagan – you must give all that up, and you must meditate as a Christian.' So he had to give up his mantra, but then he made the great discovery of John Cassian, who was one of the early Fathers. Cassian collected the teaching of the fathers of the desert, and in particular a wonderful conference on prayer by Abbot Isaac, one of the classical expressions of Christian prayer. In that, John Main discovered the Christian mantra, and their word was, 'God come to my aid, Lord make haste to help me.' Those of you who knew the Latin tradition will know it as *Deus in adjutorum meum intende, Domine ad adjuvandum me festina*. We used to chant it every day in our prayer. The idea was that in every situation, you face whatever happens. In the Eastern church this grew into the Jesus prayer. Many people are familiar with this through the wonderful little book, *The Way of a Pilgrim*, which is the story of a Russian peasant who read in the New Testament that you must pray always, pray without ceasing, and he went to various monasteries saying, 'How can I pray without ceasing?' One staretz, an elder in the monastery, taught him the prayer of Jesus. He said, 'You repeat the words, "Lord Jesus Christ, Son of God, have mercy on me a sinner," and you repeat that a thousand times, two thousand times, five thousand, you go on quietly repeating the Jesus prayer.' The man went all over Russia (in the nineteenth century, Holy Russia was like India, with holy men wandering all over the place on pilgrimage). and as he wandered the prayer went on night and day, and it transformed his life. You feel, even in his writing, that he simply radiated Christ wherever he went.

That is what we have to learn. Personally I have used the Jesus prayer for forty years now and I find it a constant standby in every situation and whatever is happening. The prayer goes on, and after a time it should become practically automatic, coming with one's breathing. The moment you sit down to meditate the prayer goes on of itself and even when you are not meditating it may start up again at any time, in a bus or a train. It keeps you in the presence of God; and prayer is the practice of the presence of God, a way of being aware of that presence day and night, wherever you are.

The Jesus Prayer was a tradition in the Eastern church from about AD 500 or 600, and it has now spread all over the world and is used by many Catholics.

John Main developed another mantra, *Maranatha*, which is Aramaic. Now Jesus spoke Aramaic, but hardly any of that Aramaic teaching survives. It was all translated into Greek. We know hardly a word that Jesus said, but there a few Aramaic words recorded in the New Testament, such as Jesus' prayer, *Abba*, 'Father'. The *Abba* prayer is very infinite, very personal, almost childlike. Jesus lived in total intimacy with the Father and expressed it in this word *Abba*. Thus you can say *Abba* was Jesus' mantra.

Then in 1 Corinithians 16:22 we find this Aramaic word *Maranatha*, 'Lord, come' (*Maran* is 'Lord', *atha* is 'come'). Incidentally, when I first went to India we joined the Seremalankara rite, which is one of the Syrian rites in Kerala coming from very early times and using Syriac, a form of Aramaic; so all our prayer was in Aramaic. I used to chant the Lord's Prayer in Aramaic, and even the words of consecration were probably very close to the original. *Ma* is 'lord', and the bishops in Kerala are called *marathanasius*, 'lord'. When applied to God, *Ma* means

Lord, *Maran* is 'Our Lord', and *ata* is 'Come, Our Lord'. You are simply invoking the presence of God. And so John Main used this when he realized that Catholics had no method of meditation. (I was a Benedictine monk from 1931 onwards, and in sixty years we never learned to meditate. We had the Divine Office, we had the Mass, and we sat to reflect and so on which was a kind of meditation but it wasn't a method of meditation. John Main introduced a method, and that is what people are looking for.)

You need some word to repeat; otherwise your mind wanders. Repeat your word and it takes you beyond your ego. We are all self-centred. Sin is self-centredness and all human beings grow up centred on themselves. The art of prayer is to get beyond the ego, beyond your self-centred personality, and be open to the transcendent. The repetition of a word, the name of God, the name of Jesus, is a way of transcending your ego. It sounds silly to be repeating some word all the time, but it is the most effective way of silencing the mind.

You sit, you breathe, you repeat your mantra, and then your mind begins all its wanderings. There are two ways of dealing with that. One is to try to still the thoughts. Some people can do that, but it is very difficult and many other people do not so much still the thoughts as observe them like clouds in the sky. Let them come and let them go; the thoughts continue at one level whilst the mantra quietly continues underneath, as it were, sustaining you in the presence of God. Gradually the thoughts will subside. Beyond all this movement of the mind is the deep centre where you are simply surrendered to God. Meditation is surrender to God. Surrender the ego; give your total self to God.

Meditation can be very frustrating. You sit down with all the best intentions and nothing happens. Your mind wanders here and there, and you seem to be wasting your time. When John Chapman was Abbot of Downside, he introduced meditation among the monks and also among lay people, and you notice when you read his very valuable *Spiritual Letters* (1935) that nearly everybody said, 'I feel I'm wasting my time. I sit there and nothing happens and my mind wanders about. I ought to do something.' And the Abbot always insisted, 'Don't "do something". Don't go and read the Bible. Sit, and give that half hour to God.' That is the essence: you take that half hour every day, morning and evening if possible, and you give that half hour to God. If he lets you have wandering thoughts all the time, or if he lets you go to sleep, you accept that, but you try to be open, to surrender to him and allow him to work in you. This is the crucial point: we can prepare ourself, we can have the body and the breath and the mind, but the prayer has to come from God. Contemplation is what we aim at. It is the activity of God, the Holy Spirit in us; it is not ourselves. St Paul says we do not know how to prayer but the Holy Spirit prays in us and that is what we are seeking. All these methods, whatever they are, are intended to bring us to the point where we are surrendered to God and we can allow the Holy Spirit to act and work in us.

Of course, that can go on endlessly. It can go on during the rest of the day. The more we surrender, the more we open ourselves, the more the Holy Spirit takes charge.

Here I would like to introduce a rather important point. We all have a body, the physical organism, and we have to learn how to harmonize the body and relate it to the world around. Then we have a psyche, a soul, and senses, feelings, imagination, reason, will, all these are faculties of the psyche; but that is not the end. Unfortunately St Paul's doctrine of body, soul, and spirit was superseded in Western thinking by the psychology of Aristotle, where the human being is simply body and soul, and many Christians still today think that a human being is body and soul. The danger of that is that you have your body and you psyche, or personality, but that is not what you are, and the trouble is that God then is somewhere 'up there'. It is a problem for many people. You project to God beyond and you pray to this God, but you are divided. But in the doctrine of St Paul the body and the soul are both united in the *pneuma*, the spirit, and our prayer must focus on the spirit, not on the body or on the psyche. The psyche is full of thoughts, feelings, desires, fears, hopes, anxieties – all these things go on in the psyche, and your ego is at the heart of your psyche, it harmonizes your psyche and that is what we have to be free from.

Only the Spirit can set us free from this world of the psyche and all its passions and desires and fears and hopes and so on. Meditation is calming the psyche, letting go of all the thoughts and feelings and becoming aware simply of the Holy Spirit; and at that point the human spirit unites with the Spirit of God and we are in communion with God. When we let the other thoughts and things go we become aware of this indwelling presence.

'The Spirit of God', says St Paul, 'joins with our spirit in testifying that we are God's children' (Rom. 8:16). At that point of the Spirit we know ourselves. Our spirit is one with the Holy Spirit and we are aware ourselves as children of God. That is what we are aiming at in meditation.

Meditation should lead to sharing the inner life of the Trinity. John Main said that to pray, to meditate, is to share in the consciousness of Christ; and the consciousness of Christ is the stream of love which flows from the Father to the Son and from the Son to the Father in the Holy Spirit. That stream of love is always flowing from the Father. Jesus is always in that communion with the Father, sharing the love and the knowledge of the Father and that knowledge and love flows out in the Holy Spirit and is communicated to us. In our meditation, when we enter that point of the Spirit, we enter into that communion of the Father and the Son in the Spirit. We enter into the inner mystery of the Godhead. Jesus wanted to share that most wonderful prayer with us. He wants us to share in his relationship to the Father. The love of the Father and the knowledge of the Father which he has in the fullness he shares with us in the Holy Spirit, so at that point of the Spirit we open upon the inner mystery of the Trinity. We come to the final absolute.

You get many disillusionments in prayer, and feel you are not getting anywhere, but you must persevere. It may take you months or weeks or years. It does not matter how long it takes, but it gradually begins to take over and the Holy Spirit begins to be more and more the centre of your life. If we are faithful in the spiritual journey, we are being led into the supreme mystery, the supreme understanding, and this is the peace which passes understanding.

People are always in confusion. So many come to our ashram and say, 'I have no peace of mind,' but when you get beyond the ego, beyond all these thoughts and so on, at the point of the Spirit you get this peace of mind, the peace which passes understanding. St Paul prays always that this peace may come. The gifts of the Holy Spirit are love, peace, and joy, and that is what we seek in meditation. They are human fulfilment. They are not fully human until we reach this level of the spirit. We are still living at a semi-human level, but when we go beyond the body and soul into the spirit, we experience the inner presence of God, the inner mystery of the godhead, and we share in the inner life of God. The path is there before us, and the goal is the absolute fulfilment of all human desire. All that is required of us really is faithfulness and perseverance and trust. God will come into your life if you trust your life to him, but you have to go on and on to the end of your life. There is no stopping on the way.

Once you have discovered the inner mystery yourself, it begins to radiate. The hope of the world, the hope of the church today, is in groups meditating, coming together day by day, week by week, year by year and gradually growing and themselves transforming, and thus transforming the world around. I pray and hope that God will help all of you to reach that point of inner experience of the mystery of God, the mystery of Christ, and be able to share it with others wherever you go.

Questions

How do you link the Ignatian emphasis on feelings with what you were saying about transcendence?

Until fairly recently the Iganatian Exercizes were almost the only method of prayer which Catholics had. I think they are extremely good as a preparation, but they are all on the discursive level. You can meditate on the Bible, and many people start with that; then you reflect on yourself, you see yourself in the light of Christ, you follow the life of Christ and all this is discursive prayer. You are using your mind and then you try to surrender yourself so you are training your will and opening to Christ, and that should lead to contemplation. St Ignatius wasn't contemplative, of course, and the Exercizes are a preliminary stage in taking people through the mind and the will and also the imagination and the senses. He used all the faculties to bring people the point where contemplation begins. Contemplation begins when the discursive line stops. It is when your mind becomes still that the divine action begins, so I see the Ignatian Exercizes as a preparation for contemplation, but they are not contemplative prayer.

What is the difference between contemplation, meditation, and reflection?

In the Middle Ages, there were four stages of prayer: *lectio, meditatio, oratio, contemplatio. Lectio*, reading the scriptures, is how most people start, and it's meditative reading, reading where you're not just reading for the information. You are trying to absorb it, take it into yourself. Then the next stage is *meditatio* in the ordinary sense, reflecting on your reading, on the gospel, on Christ, on your own inner life. Then normally meditation should lead to prayer, *oratio*. You turn to God, you ask for help, you thank God, you praise God, you recognize your sin, your need: all that is prayer, but then *lectio*, *meditatio*, and *oratio* should all lead to *contemplatio*. All through the ancient church right up to the present day, contemplation was seen as the goal of Christian life, and in contemplation your activity ceases. You have done all this, meditated and prayed, and now God begins to act in you; and that is contemplation. It is the action of the Holy Spirit praying in us. All our meditation and prayer and activity should be leading us to the point where we surrender to God and allow the Holy Spirit to act in us. Until the seventeenth century, contemplation was always understood as the goal of Christian life, not only for monks but for lay people. Then the view began to grow up that contemplation was something very special for very special people, nuns in convents and monks and so on, and ordinary people should not aspire to contemplation – they should be content with ordinary prayer, with meditation, reading, prayer, and the Mass, discursive prayer. Thus the normal lay person was cut off from the contemplative tradition. But the great Dominican theologian Père Lagrange, in his book *Contemplation and Contemplative Life*, showed that contemplation is the normal fulfilment of baptism. At baptism you receive the Holy Spirit, and in contemplation the Holy Spirit takes over, transforms your life. So then the universal call to contemplation began to be accepted, but only in this century, and not too early in this century. Now at last we realize, I think largely due to Fr John Main, that every Christian is called to contemplation. That is our goal. Often very simple people can go into contemplation if they have really surrendered to God – even if they have read very little and may not have meditated much. I'm sure many mothers of families, working all day, often reach an extraordinary state of contemplation. They have surrendered themselves to God and somehow the Holy Spirit acts in them, they get transformed.

Can you talk about the gifts of the Spirit, for example speaking in tongues?

I make a distinction between the psychic and the spiritual, which are often confused. The psychic is the higher level of the psyche and most of these gifts like speaking with tongues, healing, and all sorts of strange phenomena belong to the phenomenal world. They are appearances, outward things. They are valuable up to a point, but they are also deceptive. People get very attracted by these powers. Healing power and miracles belong to the psychic world. In India there are many holy men who perform miracles daily, but it doesn't mean much. They are psychic, not spiritual, and they can be harmful. You can use these powers for evil, and that is very common in India too. I have been amazed to find Catholic families in Madras who are under a spell from somebody – a spell is put in your garden or somewhere and you begin to get diseases and all sorts of tragedies occur. You get on to a diabolic force. So the psyche is both good and evil. The psychic powers can be very dangerous. They can be used by the Holy Spirit, and in the Acts of the Apostles there is speaking with tongues, healing and other spiritual ministeries, but it is the Spirit using these psychic powers.

The psychic is not the same as the spiritual. The Spirit can use the psyche, but the devil can use psychic powers and it is terrible when those powers are really demonic. I think Hitler was possessed by a demonic power. He was concerned with the occult, definitely, and this power was not merely human in him, it was a psychic power. These demonic forces can take possession and drive you, and many people today are under the possession of these demonic forces. Just as you can be under the possession of the angelical, the divine, so also you can get controlled by these demonic forces in the unconscious.

Do you see meditation and your prayer life as a means of coping in this world, or as a means of preparation for the next?

Obviously it has to be both, but the emphasis we give is important. I think there is a danger of living purely for the future life. As you go deeper into prayer you become more concerned with this world. There's a very famous ox picture in the Buddhist tradition: a man is going in search of an ox and he sees the traces of the ox in the sand and then he sees it in the distance and then he comes up to it and catches it by the tail and jumps on to it and he rides off into the void and the last picture is the void – he goes right beyond. Then they added another one, in which he returns to the market place. I think that in meditation you have to go beyond your personal problems, your social and political problems, and let them go; but then out of the depth of your meditation you become aware of the presence of the Holy Spirit. You have to return to the market place, you have to be aware of all the problems of the world around, even on a big scale, politically or whatever. You must always unite concern with the Absolute Transcendent One with concern for the present world. Some people, such as Mother Theresa for instance, are called to total concern for the sufferings of the poor and so on. Others may be much more concerned with the inner life and the future life, and live a solitary life; and they can be just as powerful for the church and the world. Each one has their own vocation and you have to discern how you relate the inner urge to go beyond, to surrender to God, with your concern for people and their needs. Each one must discern that for themselves.

We are warned about the use of transcendental meditation, but some people have found it helpful in their own prayer life. What is your opinion?

[52]

I think transcendental meditation is a very valuable and powerful method. Some people have worried about it because it involves mantras, which very often are the name of a Hindu god or something, but I don't think there's really anything to worry about. And incidentally, the Hindu gods are angels and demons. When a Hindu worships a god in purity, he is really worshipping God through that angel, through that spirit, so we shouldn't be anxious about that. Incidentally, at Spencer Abbey in Massachusetts they learned the mantra from transcendental meditation and brought it into their monastic Christian life. They call it 'centering prayer', and they are spreading it through parishes all over America. I think transcendental meditation is a very practical method of meditation with the mantra. It is a practical method which almost anybody can use and it can be very useful for the Christian. You can adapt it to your own need.

How do you stop yourself falling asleep when you meditate?

Abbot John Chapman always came up against that: people would say, 'Oh, you must get up and read the Bible or do something,' and he said, 'Well, if God wants them to sleep, let them sleep.' But more practically, in any meditation you often need to change your position. In Zen meditation they normally meditate for twenty-five minutes, then they get up and they do a walking meditation. I think everybody should learn that there are times when you need to change your position, maybe to walk round and so on. I think you use your discretion over that. By the way, I hope it doesn't shock you but I find reclining on a bed is an excellent way of meditation. I'm getting old and I can't sit in the lotus position any more and I find walking difficult, but when you relax and simply let go it can be beautiful, and sometimes I have been sitting for meditation and then I go and relax on the bed and a far deeper meditation comes when I'm reclining, so I recommend it – strictly for old people!

How can meditation help in marriage?

I think it can be a great help especially if both partners meditate. If one and not the other does it, it can be a bit awkward, it tends to isolate you, but if the two can meditate together I think it's wonderful. Among the people who are interested in starting an oblate community in California are a married couple who never neglect meditation morning and evening, and it's one of the strongest forces in their married life, to bring them together at a deeper level. In meditation you are beyond your sexual differences and so on. You enter into the deep, inner awareness and so your marriage is more deeply centred. Instead of being simply physical or psychological, your marriage becomes a marriage in the Spirit. That is how I would recommend all married people if they are called to it to meditate. Then your marriage is rooted in God, in the Spirit, and you are not subject to all the psychological forces which can tear you apart so easily.

Many children, too, even at the age of three or four, can learn to meditate. There is one sister who comes to our ashram and she is very, very deep in prayer and she very much wants to go to families and help children. She says if you take a very small child and tell them to say 'Jesus, I love you,' and he learns to repeat that and it becomes part of his life, it can become a real means of meditation. Small children are more open to God. They get worse as they grow older. As Wordsworth says, in his 'Ode. Intimations of Mortality',

> ... not in utter nakedness,
> But trailing clouds of glory do we come
> From God, who is our home:
> Heaven lies about us in our infancy!

The child is coming from God, and has an innocence and openness to God. Then

Shades of the prison-house begin to close
Upon the growing boy,
But he beholds the light, and whence it flows,
He sees it in his joy ...
And by the vision splendid
Is on his way attended;
At length the man perceives it die away,
And fade into the light of common day.

Children are extraordinarily open to God. I remember one lady in
America telling me about her children at the age of three, four, and
five seeing angels and having wonderful experiences and then you
go to school and all that is put down and you lose your innocence.
You can also recover it. So I think we should recognize that in married life and even among children the power of the mantra can
open anybody up to the presence of the Holy Spirit.

*Could you say something about the way people use the word 'power'
– 'the power of the Holy Spirit', 'the power of the unconscious'?*

St Paul says the gospel he proclaimed did not sway his hearers
with subtle arguments but 'by spiritual power' (1 Cor. 2:4). This
energy is working all through matter and life and all through
human beings. It is in the body, but also in the psyche. The
theory of *kundalini* is that there are *chakras,* centres of psychic
energy, in the body from the base of the spine to the crown of the
head; the centre at the base of the spine is called the *muladhara,*
and there you are in contact with all the energies of matter,
electromagnetic forces and so on, and that energy of nature is in
you? Mind you, these are dangerous. These things can take possession and drive you, but you have to learn to deal with them
and to transform them.
    Then you have the emotional centre, the *manipura* it's called,

at the navel, and most people live from the *manipura*, especially women. The feelings, the affections, are a very powerful influence in our life, and again it can be positive or it can become extremely negative. Again Hitler is a good example. He had tremendous power. A young Jewish boy came to my monastery in England in the 1930s, and he said he once went to a meeting with Hitler. Hitler talked for three hours on end and the boy said its power was overwhelming. You felt you could follow him and do whatever he wanted. He had a magnetic power – very dangerous, of course, but that is power: all these powers can become positive and be transformed.

Then you have the *anahata chakra* at the heart, and for most people that is the centre of prayer. The Fathers used to say, 'Lead the thoughts from the head into the heart and keep them there.' The heart is the source, not merely of feeling and affection, but of the mind. It is where the feelings and the affections meet the mind and come under control of the will, so it is a centre for prayer. I like to think that all the lower chakras rise up to the heart and the higher chakras descend into the heart so it becomes the centre.

Then there is the throat *chakra*, the *vishuddha*, which is for words, music, song, poetry, and creativity. The sixth *chakra*, between the eyebrows, is the *ajna*; that is the mind, where all the mental activity focusses. There is great danger in focussing on the mind. Many yogic practices focus on the mind and for some people it is all right but for people who are mentally over-developed, as many of us are, it is disastrous. You get fixed in your mental *chakra* and it simply dominates you and you lose the power of the other *chakras*.

The final one is the *sahasrara*, the thousand petal lotus at the crown of the head, and there all these energies are opened up to the transforming power beyond. The art of *kundalini* is to lead the energy through all the centres, not allowing it to go out at any level but guiding it through the centres and surrendering it to

God. That is where the power comes, and many of the saints had miraculous powers because the energies had been transformed by the Holy Spirit and were flowing out in the power of the Spirit.

So power is at every level and is positive and negative. It can become terribly negative and disastrous, and the same negative power can become positive and creative and transforming. We all have to try to learn to experience this power of the Spirit to transform the whole personality, opening it up to God. Being in communion with the Holy Spirit and is the power we all need.

You talked about contemplation coming back into the market place. Can you share with us something about perceptions which contemplation gives you as you come back into the market place? I'm really asking a question about God and politics.

As we open ourselves to prayer and to the presence of the Holy Spirit, it should penetrate our practical life; it can also penetrate political life, and the key to that is detachment. The central teaching of the *Bhagavad Gita*, that wonderful spiritual guide which I recommend to everybody, is detachment. As long as you are in your ego, your self centre, everything you do is corrupted. Your ego gets into everything, even the most spiritual prayer. Charitable works can all be centred through your ego, satisfying your personality, and it becomes a negative force. But if you detach the ego from your self centre and surrender to God, then all the energies of your nature can be used in the power of the Spirit. The Spirit's power gives you discernment in politics and in economics, to understand the ordering of society and so on. What we need today is men of spiritual vision of that kind, and they are very, very rare; if they do get it, they don't get into politics. (I'm very keen on Jerry Brown, one of the 1992 presidential candidates in America. He's a very interesting man who was Governor of California for two terms and when he was standing for noination as Democratic candidate for President I had a long talk with him. His chances of getting in were small – he had no money or anything – but he was a very intelligent, deeply spiritual man who had been a Jesuit seminarian for some time. I said to him, 'You should stand for spirituality in political, economic life.' We really do need knowledge of economics and the whole political world, but it should be under the guidance of a higher wisdom, and once you gain an awareness of the presence of God the Holy Spirit, it should give you discernment in politics, in economics, in whatever you are doing. In our ashram most people are engaged in work of some kind, and they come to discover a deeper centre from which they can work in their particular service of the world. Notice that it is said that Jesus went into Galilee 'with the power of the Spirit' (Luke 4:14). Six weeks in the desert meditating, praying, open to God, and then 'armed with the power of the Spirit' he went preaching. That is our model.

John Main said that when you meditate you must stress the four syllables and pay attention to those; is what you are suggesting different?

This is two different ways of understanding the mantra and it's quite important. John Main as you say, insisted simply on repeating the word and was not concerned with the meaning very much. Many Hindu teachers have the same method. For them the mantra is more the sound, and you tune into that sound and it centres you and you vibrate with it and enter into deep meditation. I think that is perfectly valid, and for many people it may be the best way, but I have always been drawn to the opposite. I have always felt the mantra should be a prayer, should have a meaning, and that is why I use the Prayer of Jesus. I think the two go together: a mantra without any vibration of sound, without any sort of psychological power like that, would be very defective, but I do feel if you simply keep it on the level of the sound of the word, it can be rather limiting. To me, if you open it up to the Holy Spirit, to Christ, and to the Father, it seems to open up the mantra to a deeper level; but that is just my experience.

Can you say something about the word Om?

The word *Om* has no specific meaning. It is a bit like 'Amen' – it might even be connected with it, for it is often spelt *aum.* The Hindu tradition is that it is the word which comes out of the soul in the silence, so it is a primordial word from which the whole creation comes. It is a very sacred mantra. Many Hindus use the word. In the Apocalypse Jesus is said to be the Alpha and the Omega, the first and the last letter of the alphabet, and in the Indian tradition we say *Om*, the word which comes from the silence of the Father, so it has a very deep meaning.

Can you talk about suffering, particularly emotional suffering and that unfortunate hang-up of Western society, material suffering?

We are all exposed to suffering in some way, and some of us very acutely. We have to learn how to accept suffering and make it a means of openness to God. Of course in a sense it is the heart of the gospel. Jesus accepted the total suffering and humiliation of the cross, and through that he was able to make his total surrender, so suffering is very important in that it has a positive value. Sometimes we feel that suffering is just negative: we must get rid of it, take medicine and go to a doctor, get clear of it by all means. That is all very well at a certain level, but we have to learn to accept suffering. When Jung was working as a psychologist, he said that the majority of people who came to him in their early forties were suffering now because they had refused to suffer in the past. You keep putting suffering away, you won't accept it, and it reaches a point where you can't bear it any longer and it breaks you. We must learn to accept suffering in small ways, as Thérèse of Lisieux did. You accept little sufferings as they come day by day, getting near to seeing them as gifts of God.

I remember once walking with a great disciple of Gandhi. He walked all over India getting people to give land to the poor, and he had an abdominal ulcer. 'This is my gift,' he said of it. The pain of that was a constant reminder to him of his human need, his human weakness and of the need for prayer. So suffering is also the gift of God, awakening you beyond your ego and opening you.

Once suffering is accepted as coming from God, the will of God, it becomes creative; but all the time you resist it and drive it away, it gets more and more negative and becomes unbearable half the time. We all have to learn to bring the suffering into our meditation. You will hear teachers say that when you are sitting meditating it gets very painful after a time, and you should not try to get rid of the pain but observe it. This means trying to detach your mind from your body and simply observe it. Often, apparently, the pain goes away altogether.

We all have to deal with suffering and some people – permanent invalids and so on – are suffering all the time. Learning to accept suffering and to surrender to it can be a means of meditation. It is a way of opening the heart to God and experiencing the Holy Spirit. I am not very good at it, but I think it is something we all need to learn how to deal with.

You were talking about the divisions of religion. If we accept the existence of one God and feel in tune with the one God, is religion then necessary?

I'm afraid that doesn't work. Buddhists don't believe in one God at all. The Buddhists have a great problem. They have no God and yet they are the most devout people, so I think the one God is really a problem. The Jews have it, the Moslems have it and the Christians have it but the Oriental does not have this belief in one God.

I recommend a wonderful little book called *A Taste of Water*, by a Jesuit, Thomas Hand, and a Chinese sister, Chuen Lee (Paulist Press, 1990). The Jesuit spent most of his life in Japan and the faith of their book is Christianity from the point of Taoism and Buddhism – a Chinese religion, if you like. There is no God, but a sense of the pervading Spirit. The whole universe is pervaded by the Spirit: it pervades your whole human life: it pervades your inner person and you are playing with the Spirit, the Taoist flow of life, of energy, of divine life. It comes to the same thing in the end but they do not believe in one God at all; the one God is really a Semitic religion. Others have a deep sense of pervading the universe, pervading all human life, pervading human consciousness and at the same time transcending it; but they don't name it as God and the Buddha absolutely refused to name God. He says as soon as you start talking about it you start quarrelling about this God and that God, so he said you should not think or talk about it at all but surrender yourself it. God has no name. We think we have got it, the God we know now, but it is simply a projection. St Thomas Aquinas was extremely clear about this. All our images and concepts are immeasurably short of the reality. We talk as though we know God and we want to tell people about God, but it is our God, our projection, our image. It can be very helpful, but it is limited. God himself remains beyond all this. So I think the idea of the one God and the Father of all is all very well for Semitic people but not for Oriental people. I think we have to go beyond the one God to what I call the Divine Mystery, which is present everywhere and is present in any form of God – the names and forms have behind them the nameless and formless One who transcends all.

If you accept the Divine Mystery, is religion necessary?

Religion is an expression of the Divine Mystery in human terms. To me, all religion centres on a transcendent Mystery which cannot be named. It has no form and yet is the meaning of all human existence. We need to express it in name and words and thoughts and images and doctrines, and each religion expresses the Divine Mystery in its own language; each has its own value and its own insight and each has its own meditations. We have to realize that Christianity is an expression of the Divine Mystery in the context of a Semitic religion, of a particularly Jewish community, and Jesus uses the language of that Semitic people and that Jewish community. It is a unique revelation within that particular context; we have to recognize that the Divine Mystery expressed itself in India and in China in a quite different way, but it is the one Divine Mystery present and communicating itself and drawing people everywhere in every situation. That to me is the only way to answer this problem of different religions.

You mentioned baptism as being a universal call to contemplation. The church also says that through our baptism we are called to evangelize the world. How do you see that?

That is one of the limitations of the Christian tradition. We have our particular initiation ceremony of baptism and it is valid for all Christians, but for the vast number of people it has no meaning. Sacraments belong to the world of signs. The Divine Mystery communicates itself through signs, physical or verbal, and baptism is one of the signs by which the Divine Mystery communicates itself, so it has value as a sign for those who are Christians; but for those who are not it has none. It is very like circumcision for the Jews. Paul addressed the problem of whether people ought to be circumcized. The Jews were all circumcised. Jesus himself was a

Jew, circumcized on the eighth day, and many of the early Christians thought it was obvious that all Christians should be circumcized. But Paul saw that this was simply a particular dispensation for the Jews and that it had no validity for those outside. He could do away with circumcision.

I feel we have to present our own Christian faith with its values and its limitations, and listen to others with their particular faith and their particular understanding. We grow through this dialogue, this meeting. Evangelization without dialogue is meaningless. It's no good preaching the gospel to people when they are not ready to receive it. First of all you have to talk with them.

I have a good example of this. When I first came to India we had a little ashram outside Bangalore, and Hindu students began to come, out of curiosity. We had the Upanishads, the *Bhagavad Gita*, and so on. They were extremely interested to know that we knew much more about it than they did, of course, so they were really very interested, and then spontaneously they would begin to ask about the life of Christ. If you show interest in other people, and try to understand their religion, then they are interested in your religion and want to listen to you, but if you start by trying to put your religion on to them they just turn away. In India it's terrible – people hate Christians, you know. They feel that evangelization, proselytization, is aggression – a particularly Western aggression – against their culture, against their religion. They won't listen to you. I remember one Indian Catholic telling me he once invited his many Hindu friends to hear an evangelist. This evangelist said, 'There's only one God, only one Christ, only one religion. We must all be in Christ.' None of the Hindus reacted at all. The next day he asked them why, and they said they had heard all that before. It meant nothing to them at all. But if you open yourself to them and see how they stand towards God, then it becomes deeply meaningful. Then the gospel gathers meaning and value for them. Dialogue is essential to all evangelization.

Coming back to the practical aspects of meditation, should we be trying to harmonize the use of the mantra with our breathing?

Personally, I very much believe in that. We sit and breathe, and if you let the mantra go with the breathing it enters into the whole body, into the whole of your being, so you pray with your whole breathing. I personally always take the mantra with the breathing, and I recommend it to everybody, though some people tell me that it confuses them, and they prefer simply to repeat the word. I think you must find your own way, but for those for whom it works then certainly to repeat the mantra with the breathing is a very powerful way of meditation.

Do you agree that yoga meditation does not lead people to God?

God has very little place in yoga – in Patanjali particularly. You can use it if you like; it's a more elementary, basic method concerned more with the body and the breathing and the control of the mind; but in the deeper yoga which is taken up by other schools it's used as a means for opening the heart and the mind to the transcendent. I see yoga really as a preparatory discipline, very valuable as far as it goes, but also very limited and not necessary; but many people find that because we do not control our bodies properly and are not aware of them, it can be very helpful. But it is only a means which opens us up to the deeper prayer, the deeper meditation, and eventually to contemplation; by itself it is not sufficient at all.

The church

I would like to reflect a little on the nature of the church. What I say may shock some people, I don't know, but I think we need to reflect on it and to remind ourselves of these terrible divisions.

I mentioned my friend from Northern Ireland. She has said it is horrifying where everyone is absolutely convinced they are right and the other people are wrong – and it has gone on for centuries. It is a kind of disease, or a collective ego. The individual ego is not enough, you now have a collective ego and you're convinced that you alone have the truth and everybody else must be wrong.

I see a way round this if we reflect on the origin of the church. Biblical studies today make it perfectly clear that the institutional church as we know it – the hierarchy, the sacraments, the dogmas, the law – began in the second century. It emerged from the first century but it really only got structured in the second century. There were no bishops in the first century. Jesus appointed the apostles, and the apostles appointed bishops; but biblical studies today make it absolutely clear that there were no bishops in our sense in the first century. They emerged in the second century. By the time of St Ignatius of Antioch, it is very clear that the bishop, as head of the diocese, becomes the basis of the whole organization, but in the first century there were people called presbyters, or elders, and there were also *episcopi*, 'bishops', but they were not the head of any church. There is no mention of bishops or priests in the letters to the Corinthians or the Ephesians written in the fifties and sixties.

According to the leading Catholic bibilical scholar Raymond Brown, Jesus founded a community, the twelve apostles, with

Peter at their head, and he entrusted the message of the kingdom of God to that community and he gave the Holy Spirit to that community and he left it to the Holy Spirit to guide that community to organize itself and to develop its doctrine and its law. There is no evidence that there were bishops or priests or dogmas or sacraments or any of the institutional church as we know it until at least the end of the first century.

Interestingly, in the second century the Roman church was not held to be founded by Peter but by Peter and Paul. This is a very strong tradition; it goes into our liturgy, Peter and Paul, the founders of the church, and what appears now is that Peter and Paul were martyred in Rome in the sixties and by their witness of martyrdom they were considered to be the spiritual founders of the Roman church. That gave the Roman church tremendous authority. St Irenaeus, writing at the end of the second century, said, 'If you want to be sure of the Christian faith, go to Rome. That is the church of the apostles Peter and Paul and there the true faith is always preserved.' So the Roman church emerged from the apostolic college founded by Jesus, and it developed historically in the Graeco-Roman world. From the second century on it was seen as the centre of Christendom, having its source in the apostles Peter and Paul.

Biblical scholars today recognize three stages in the composition of the New Testament. The first is Jesus' preaching in Palestine. We know that he taught in the synagogues in Galilee and went up to Jerusalem. In a synagogue the Bible was read in Hebrew, but after the exile in 500 bc the Jews no longer spoke Hebrew; they spoke Aramaic, a dialect of Hebrew which spread all over the Middle East. In the synagogue they would read the Old Testament in Hebrew and interpret it in Aramaic. So when Jesus read the prophecy of Isaiah in the synagogue, he would have read it in Hebrew, but his commentary on it would have been in Aramaic. All Jesus' teaching was in Aramaic, but only a few phrases have survived, such as when he raises the little girl and

says, ' "*Talitha cum*", which means, "Get up, my child" ' (Mark
5:41). The vast majority of Jesus' teaching as we have it is transla-
tions. Jesus did not intend to leave any words behind. If he had, we
would have idolized the words; we would have said, 'Stick to these
words, this is the Word of God, you can't change it at all.' But he
left no words behind. He left the Holy Spirit behind to guide the
church into all truth, but no words.

The next phase, from AD 30 to 60, the story of Jesus was
handed down in the churches, first of all in Aramaic. Then, of
course, as the church spread to Antioch and the Greek cities, the
original gospel of Jesus was translated into Greek and passed
down in the churches in various different forms. There must have
been many. St Luke in the beginning of his Gospel says that he
consulted many written accounts of the gospel.

Then from AD 60 to 90 as the apostles passed away there was a
need of a written gospel. Before that they didn't really need it.
There were reliable witnesses who spoke the language and were
able to interpret it. And so from 60 to 90 our written Gospels came
into being, all written in Greek, translated from the Aramaic – and
of course, when you translate you interpret, you can't help it. So
each Gospel interprets the message of Jesus in its own way and
each has its own characteristics.

We are able now to compare one with another and we see the
different point of view from which they write. As each has its own
value, each has its own limitations. At the end of this period, in AD
90, came the Gospel of John, almost certainly written at Ephesus,
which was a centre of gnosticism, a divine wisdom which probably
comes from India through Persia to Egypt and then into the whole
of the Mediterranean world. The Gospel of John interpreted the
original oral gospel in the light of this gnostic wisdom, thus giving
the Palestinian gospel a broader dimension. That is why it begins
with the *Logos*. The *Logos* was the word which was used in the
gnostic tradition for the divine wisdom, so Jesus is seen as the
manifestation of the divine wisdom. John goes deeper into the

mystery of Jesus and reveals the inner life of Jesus in a way that had not been done before. All the Gospels undoubtedly go back to Jesus himself, but we never know exactly what he said; they are always to some extent interpretations in the context of their own situation, their own understanding. It was when the churches began to organize themselves that the four Gospels were seen to be the authentic witness and became part of the New Testament.

I don't think Jesus established a historical church – he left that to come into being in the course of time. He did establish the church of the Spirit, the eschatalogical church, the church of the end times, and all through the gospel Jesus speaks about the coming end. He is always preparing them for the Second Coming, telling them that the end would come and all would be fulfilled. Our divisions come from the institutional church – the Roman church, and then other churches that were rivals to Rome, and the churches of Antioch, Alexandria, and so on. All the differences emerge through the written Gospel, the written language. When you put the message into words and thoughts and structures, then it begins to change and vary. The gospel itself is beyond the Gospels. They are written witnesses, but they are witnessing to the original message which is not in words. You don't believe in the Gospels, you believe in the divine mystery which was revealed in the gospel. It comes the form of the written Gospels, but Jesus himself remains behind it all. Our faith is not in the Gospels, it is in Jesus. Christian faith is not in any words or thoughts or language or doctrine, it is in the divine mystery, the divine person, from whom all this language, all these doctrines emerge. All doctrines, dogmas, sacraments, hierarchy, all the organization of the church is a manifestation in historic times. So the differences emerge from the original unity; they are perfectly natural, historical growth, but all are historically conditioned.

The Catholic church is not the original Palestinian church but is basically a Graeco-Roman church which was been developed in Europe in the Middle Ages. It has a definite historical, linguistic, social, psychological base but the original church, the original mystery, is beyond all these structures, all these forms.

Now take the Trinity. The word 'Trinity' does not appear in the Gospels at all. It is a word and a thought which emerged in the Graeco-Roman world. The whole structure of doctrine was in terms of Greek theology. All the words used in theology are Greek words translated into Latin. 'Trinity', 'incarnation' and so on are all Greek words, all expressing the divine mystery in the context of Graeco-Roman culture.

The Graeco-Roman world opened up Europe, and then all the barbarian peoples, from the fifth to the tenth century, destroyed the Roman Empire and the Graeco-Roman church developed under the influence of their understanding; thus the church of the Middle Ages emerged.

Then, of course, came the Reformation where the people saw how far the church had grown from its original basis in Palestine. Protestants wanted to return to the Bible, get rid of all this Graeco-Roman and Teutonic development, and find the original gospel and the Bible. So the Protestants rejected all this development of the church and went back to the Bible, not realizing that the Bible itself was a particular development of the teaching of Jesus and that they were interpreting his life in the light of their own under-standing. We always read in the light of our own understanding; to get back to the original gospel is impossible. You cannot get back to the original actually, but the Protestant religion is based on the Bible and it is a wonderful interpretation of the Bible and is one way of expressing Christian faith.

So each of these is a particular way of expressing the Christian faith. Each is valid in its own way, and I see no reason to deny that the Holy Spirit is present. I believe it was present in the Roman church developing its doctrine and its law; its whole system is a development of the original mystery of Christ, the original mystery of the church growing through history with its ups and downs, its negative and positive character, growing and guided in history by the Spirit. The same must be said of Orthodoxy. The Orthodox have churches just as ancient as the church of Rome. The church of Antioch was founded even before the church of Rome, so they feel that they have the original Christian faith; but again it comes down to them mainly through the Greek tradition. The Roman church, of course, developed the Latin and Eastern Europe the Greek tradition, so they have an authentic expression of the gospel expressed in Greek and the neighbouring Slavonic. It is one way of expressing the gospel in liturgy and theology and canon law.

Each of these churches claims to be the final truth. The Council of Florence in the sixteenth century stated that outside the Roman church no one could be saved, whether pagans or Jews or heretics or schismatics; they would all go to the eternal fire prepared for the devil and his angels unless they entered the Roman church. That is the original Roman doctrine. We have gone round it now, made reservations and so on, but it has never been withdrawn and that was a terrible division, rejecting everybody. The Orthodox have done the same, as have the Protestants. I think we must admit that each church has its own value. I would not deny the Holy spirit to any branch of Christianity. As long as there is genuine faith and hope and love it creates a church in which the Holy Spirit is present but, of course, there are great limitations. Personally, as a Catholic I believe that the Holy Spirit guides the Roman church in all its development and that in spite of many errors and many disasters on the way, the Holy Spirit is present; but I don't think we should deny it to the other churches. Wherever people have faith and hope and love and are open to the Spirit they get some guidance from the Holy Spirit. We have to learn to respect one another, not to condemn one another but to recognize the Spirit's presence.

The one thing that Jesus gave to the church was the Holy Spirit. He would be present among his disciples in the Holy Spirit. He is present wherever people meet with faith and love in his name (Matt. 18:20); something of the Holy Spirit, the Word of God, comes through all our different traditions. But now we need to go beyond all these divisions and recognize that all traditions have their source in the Holy Spirit, given to the disciples by Jesus himself, uniting us in and through him with the Father. The eternal church, to which we all belong, is that communion of the disciples of Jesus in the Spirit through knowledge of the Son uniting us together with the Father. Thus we recognize the original, eschatalogical church of the Spirit from which all the churches derive. Our faith is not in any particular organization but in the divine mystery itself, revealed in Jesus and communicated through the Spirit to the churches. All expressions of the mystery in language or ritual or doctrine are developments, manifestations of the original church which has no name or form. Ultimate reality has no name or form. It takes name and form as we talk about it and try to describe it, but the reality itself is beyond; the original church in which we all breathe has no name and form. It is the church of the Spirit, it is the divine mystery itself present among us.

Jesus was a layman, not a priest; nor were the apostles priests. Jesus commissioned the apostles to preach the kingdom of God, to heal, and to save by the power of the Holy Spirit. Jesus was a Rabbi wandering through the villages of Galilee with a group of disciples and surrendering everything – very like a Hindu *sanyasin* who renounces his home and family. Often the *sanyasin* will renounce his name, and if you ask him where he comes from he will say, 'I've come from God.' The *sanyasin* has no settled dwelling and is not supposed to ask for any money or food for himself. It is still quite common in India to see a *sanyasin* standing outside a house, waiting for whoever will give him some food. Most devout householders always keep some rice to offer to a *sanyasin* – they prostrate themselves and touch the *sanyasin*'s feet, revering God in him. That was like Jesus and his disciples, who preached the Kingdom of God wandering through the villages with no settled dwelling.

India has been a revelation to me of the gospel. In Europe today you cannot do without money, provisions, and a car, but in India you can be totally simple. A *sanyasin* has two garments, a garment round the waist and a garment round the shoulders or over the head of unstitched cloth. There is nothing else. He wanders barefoot through the villages and simply stays wherever any householder invites him; or sometimes he goes to a temple and will stay there. He is totally dependent on divine providence. I have known some wonderful people who simply surrender to God like that and wander through the villages and accept what is given them in food and cloth or rest or whatever it may be.

I think that was the original church of Jesus and his disciples and I feel this is a kind of model for us. Many people today are feeling that the church is too institutionalized; it is so organized and structured that it is difficult to get behind it. This is a real problem. In Spain, which is supposed to be the most Catholic country in the world, they say only ten per cent of the people go to Mass now. It is the same in Germany. Even the Italians never go to church except on a festive occasion. They want Christ, they want the gospel, but the organized structure with its rather out-of-date ceremonies and language simply puts people off today.

The people who come to our ashram tell me, one after another, 'Until I was fifteen I went to church and went to Mass. I was an ordinary Catholic. After that, I gave up the whole thing.' They want to find the true church, the true Christ, the true living gospel, but it is very difficult to find in the churches as they are. I think we have to look beyond the structured churches. They have their place – we need the sacraments, we need the Mass obviously, we need the hierarchy, we need the organization – but they are a means, not an end. They are something that takes us on our way, and we always go beyond the structured and institutional church to the original, the mystery of Christ, the mystery of the church which is so powerful in the letter to the Ephesians. So I think we have to look beyond the organized church to the church of the Spirit which is behind and within the organized churches and that is the church of lay people.

As I've said, Jesus and his disciples were a lay community – and incidentally, for those interested in monastic life, St Benedict was a layman, and so were all the early Benedictine monks. They were lay communities, then priesthood came in, particularly in the town, where the need for a priest was felt. Gradually it became part of the system that monks were ordained as priests, but they did not choose to be priests, it was simply part of the system. Nowadays we are trying to realize that priesthood is a unique vocation and with a particular sacramental ministry to people; the monastic life is not necessarily a priestly vocation at all, but is total surrender to God and union with God. St Benedict asked, 'Does he truly seek God?' – that is the call of the monk, not to be a minister or preach.

So behind the organized church and priesthood, sacraments and so on, is the church of the people, the *laos*, the people of God. Right through the Old Testament and into the New, we find these people of God, a holy people, a chosen nation. That is the *laos*, and I think the call of the church today is the call of the laity.

John Main was a monk at Ealing Abbey. A group of lay people began to come to the monastery to meditate, and he taught them to meditate with the mantra. They formed a little lay community and then people began to meditate in their homes; and so this lay movement grew up with people seeking God in their daily life in the world. That is where I think the future lies. I think monasteries still have their place, particularly in guiding and helping oblates, who are attached to monasteries but are lay people living independent lives dedicated to love in the world. People want a dedicated life, particularly in America. They do not want to go into a convent or a monastery, and they do not want just an ordinary married life. They want a dedicated life as married people or as single people. I have a great belief in oblate communities, communities of lay men and women dedicated to God in prayer and meditation. (Priests can join them but only as members with the rest.) They go on living in their different ways, but every morning and evening they meet and they meditate and focus their whole life in union with God. This is open to anybody. Circumstances vary tremendously, and for many people it is difficult. The more common thing is for people to lead their own lives at home and to meet together for meditation once, twice, or three times a week. Many are doing that all over the world, but others are coming to form communities, living together in some place with the centre around prayer and meditation but at the same time earning their living in different ways.

Secular life today offers so little and is so fragmented. If only you can live your secular life dedicated to God in prayer and meditation day by day, morning and evening, then your life has new meaning and power and purpose. In doing that, we discover a sort of a lay order in the church. Just as the apostles themselves were lay people, so people today are being called. We keep in touch with the church, naturally, in the sacraments and so on, but we go beyond it. In our daily life we are part of the lay people of God, with Jesus himself as our model. He had the priesthood of Melchisedech, an eternal priesthood, but he was not a priest in the Levitical sense, and so he is the model for all of us of our total surrender to God. He teaches us how to free ourselves from our bonds of attachment and so on, open our hearts to God, and whilst earning our own living to consecrate our lives to God, in prayer and meditation.

I hope these lay communities will grow and become a living force in the church and be much more than the traditional monastic and religious communities. Many religious communities are simply fading away, particularly in Europe. There are huge novitiates completely empty. That kind of life had its very great value in the church: it has given saints to the church again and again, and it still has a value for some people, but for fewer and fewer. Yet the urge for spiritual life, for giving one's life to God, is growing everywhere among lay people.

I once visited about fifteen monasteries in America, and then a year or two later they invited me to come again and in Kansas City they invited monks and others to come and share together, and I think half a dozen monks came, most from one monastery. Nobody else took any notice of it – but there were about twenty or thirty sisters and there were one hundred and fifty lay people. It is lay people who are looking for an experience of God in prayer and meditation, so I feel this is the way the church is moving. We are moving out of a clerical system and beyond religious organizations to the lay community dedicated to God in prayer and meditation.

Of course, living a life of surrender to God and yet earning one's living in the world has its problems. It is not easy to balance the two. But this way of 'lay monks' goes back to Jesus himself and has a very deep meaning today.

Questions

Can you say something about the absence of women? Why didn't Christ choose any women as disciples?

Women had a very important place in the life of Jesus. He was obviously at home with Mary and Martha; they were very close friends. And Mary Magdalene, of course, was the first apostle, the first person to preach the gospel. She, a woman, brought the news of the resurrection. It's amazing when you think of it. Jesus obviously was changing the tradition about women. He was totally open to them, to their presence, and had women as close friends; there were women among Jesus' chosen disciples, and wherever he went through the villages the women accompanied him. You find it in St Luke's Gospel particularly. As women always do, they provided the coffee and the meals, they looked after the disciples; so it was not men alone. Jesus chose men and women to be his disciples and they went round with him preaching the gospel.

In the early church, there were no priests to begin with. There were very varied ministries: apostles and prophets, various teachers and helpers and administrators and so on. Obviously it was a loosely organized community, it was a communion of the Spirit, but the Spirit chose people with their gifts to minister in their different ways and there were both men and women among these leaders in the church. It is not conspicuous, I admit, and men seem to tend to dominate, but you do find that in all Paul's letters he writes at the end, addressing people, and mentions particularly women who are fellow workers in the gospel and to whom he owed so much. In Romans 16:15 he mentions someone called Junia, or Julia; people originally supposed that she was a male, but now it is well established that she was a female, and she is called an apostle. There were many ministries in the early church, according to need; and both men and women shared those ministries.

I think that is the direction the church is moving in today. The priesthood will go, the male priesthood that has dominated the whole church; and now, I think, we are beginning to see that we do not need women priests. That would be putting the priesthood back. We need a diversity of ministries where men and women work together in the service of the kingdom of God. That, I feel, is the model for the church. It is actually happening in many places. In America, I know, there is a shortage of priests everywhere, and very often a parish will be run by a group of people, maybe a priest and one or two men and women. Women do half the work, taking communion, reading the lessons and the intercessory prayers, and always distributing communion. So women are coming now more and more to ministry in the church. We are moving out of the very clericalized system of male priests and are beginning to discover how men and women together are called to the ministry of the church. It will evolve gradually but it is already taking place in many ways. There is great hope for women in the church, but the present system is terribly limited – we all admit that women have very little say in the church at present.

What do you think of the wider ecumenism as taught by Matthew Fox, going beyond the different Christian denominations and between all the religions?

Matthew Fox doesn't take it very far at present. It is more among American Indians, or native Americans. He is very interested in them and their cosmic religion, a religion of God's presence in the earth, in the water, in the air, in the animals, in the plants and in human beings and ancestors; and that is part of our tradition really. That sort of presence of God in nature has been put down a lot. We have tended to focus always on God's presence in Christ, and neglected his presence in creation, in matter, and in life. Matthew Fox is trying to bring that back into the church, and I think he is doing a great work.

I don't think he goes very far into religious dialogue yet, he's on that way, and I think that is our next stage. As we learn to respect different Christian churches and see the presence of Christ in each, we have to learn to see the presence of the Word of God and the Spirit of God in every genuine religion. The Gospel of John says, 'In the beginning was the Word, and the Word was with God, and the Word was God ... without him was not anything made that was made,' and then it says, 'The true light that enlightens every man was coming into the world' (John 1:1, 3, 9, RSV). Every human receives light from the Word; we receive it in the depths of our being, in the depths of the Spirit. An atheist who believes in justice, in truth, in honesty and care for others – such a person is responding to the Word of God. The Word of God is present in all humanity and in the heart of every person. And with the Word is the Spirit; the Word gives light, the Spirit gives power. The Spirit of God is present everywhere in nature. Whenever human beings are working together, sharing together, trying to live out life in relation to God, this power of the Spirit is present, and so I think we have to admit that in every religion, outside every religion, there is this presence of the Word and the presence of the Spirit in Christ.

[77]

The church is a focus as it were: Jesus is the Word made flesh, the fullness of that Word is present in him, and is present in some way everywhere.

Jesus was filled with the Holy Spirit, but that Spirit is present also everywhere. Jesus is the focus, the centre: we are all gathered in him, but the power and grace from the Spirit are everywhere and we have to respect it in every person and every religion and outside every religion. God has a much wider vision than we have. After all, human beings were in this world for tens of thousands of years before Jesus was born, and God was there in all the ancient religions, so God was present with his Word, his Spirit, in varying forms. There are many imperfections and so on, but he is always present. He has never left humanity without guidance, without some light. The presence is everywhere, and for us that presence and that power is focussed in Christ, but it is not limited; it is present everywhere, but it has its fullness and centre and final fulfilment in Jesus.

What would you say is the rôle of the Eucharist in the Christian community?

That is a matter of symbolism. The symbol is a sign by which reality becomes present to human consciousness. Suzanne Langer wrote a wonderful book called *Philosophy in a New Key*, which impressed me immensely. She says that the whole sense world around us is a world of signs by which reality (God if you like) becomes present to our consciousness.

Every word is a symbol, a sign. Take the word 'tree', or 'calf', or whatever – it is a sign by which the reality of a tree or calf becomes present to my consciousness. We live in a world of symbols, and all religious doctrines are symbolic. When we talk about the Father, the Son, the Spirit becoming flesh in the redemption, we are using human language, signs, which point to and make present this divine reality. One of my favourite hymns is 'Adoro te devote, latens Deitas', by St Thomas Aquinas:

> O Christ, whom now beneath a veil we see,
> May what we thirst for soon our portion be:
> To gaze on thee unveiled, and see thy face,
> The vision of thy glory and thy grace.

In the theology of St Thomas Aquinas the word *sacramentum* means 'sign', and for him the *sacramenta* are the bread and the wine. They are signs, and the thing signified is the body and blood of Christ which is present under the sign. We enter the presence of Christ under the signs of bread and wine. St Thomas says that the thing signified by the Eucharist, apart from the *sacramentum*, is the unity of the body of Christ, and when we partake of the Eucharist we enter into the community of the body of Christ, the mystical body of Christ. We sometimes speak of the Eucharist as the mystical body of Christ. It's not Jesus in his human body and blood. It is Jesus in the fullness of his divine life radiated throughout the world. So when we share the Eucharist we enter into the mystical body of Christ, members of that body sharing his life, his death, and his resurrection. It is all the mystery under the signs and this is very important. I think some people have too literal a sense, so transubstantiation is a bit of a problem. Many people think it means a substance in the modern sense but it does not. In the medieval view, 'substance' is what underlies all the outward appearances of a thing and answers the question 'What is it?' I see a piece of bread and ask 'What is it?' and you say, 'It is bread.' Then in transubstantiation the 'What is it?' – the thing signified by the outward form – is the body and blood of Christ, so when I see the consecrated host and wine and ask, 'What is it?', you say that it is not simply bread, it is the body and blood of Christ. The symbol is the sign by which the reality (in the case of the Eucharist, the real presence of Christ) becomes present to us. That is the theology of St Thomas.

The sacraments came in the second century. Surely you wouldn't apply that to the Body of Christ which St Paul refers to in his letter to the Corinthians? You wouldn't say that was to come in the second century, would you?

No, it was the *organization* of the sacrament that began then. The *doctrines* of the sacrament were all present in nucleus, if you like. The way we celebrate the Mass is incredibly different from what it was. It seems clear Jesus had the custom of celebrating a sacred meal with his disciples. Taking bread and wine was part of that sacred meal, a shared meal. Basically the Eucharist is a meal shared together. The day before his passion, Jesus took the bread and the wine and gave it this unique significance. 'This is my body ... this is my blood.' So the sacrament was instituted by Jesus and the apostles celebrated it in the same way. They met together and shared a meal together, and during the meal they took the bread and the wine and they saw that as a particular sign of the presence of Jesus among them. So the sacrament was basically present as doctrine: the Trinity, the Incarnation, and redemption were all present but they were not organized, systematized, and categorized until the second century. It's the organization of the church that appears in the second century; the embryo, the basis, was present from the time of Jesus. It all goes back to him originally but not in the form in which we receive it. The way we celebrate the Mass, the way we express our theology, is a development in the Graeco-Roman world.

Why are there relatively few younger people interested in contemplation? Can you suggest any remedies?

I think it takes time and maturity before you get beyond the fascination of knowledge and science and technology – all the things you can learn – and come to a deeper awareness. In India today there is a strong tradition of meditation, but all the young people are fascinated by science and technology and medicine and engineering. It is only as you attain a certain maturity that you begin to turn within and discover the deeper reality.

Is it not more a question of a lack, of disillusionment among young people rather than lack of maturity?

I think you may be right. I think young people are very disillusioned with the church because of its kind of conventional language and ritual. I took to it naturally, but it doesn't seem to answer to their needs. It's all strange to them, unreal, and that is probably the reason why so many of them won't go to Mass any more. Maybe they haven't realized the deeper meaning of it but the whole ritual alienates people. Instead of drawing them to Christ we tend to alienate them, and then they try to become Hindus or Buddhists. They try to have some inner life, and then when they find it they often come back to the church. Reality is there, but somehow it doesn't come out in the ordinary church service, at least for many people.

Why was it that in the later church prayer became identified with just intellectual discursive prayer and the Spirit got locked out?

It was a historical evolution, I think. The medieval world was extraordinarily literate. They were all reading books and studying Greek and Latin literature. The more spontaneous movement of the Spirit seemed to have gone, and this more literary, intellectual approach prevailed and was supported by the organization of the church. It is much easier to organize theology and liturgy and things like that than to organize the Spirit. The Spirit won't be organized, and so the mystical tradition always tends to go into the background and the intellectual doctrine and the ritual begins to take over; but that is just human nature. It is easier to put things into language and doctrines and rituals than to experience the Spirit. Today, for many people, ritual and doctrine are no longer attractive. We are called to experience what lies behind it all in the mystery of Christ.

I have visited several lay communities recently and in each case they have to import a priest once a week from outside the community to support them and give them the Eucharist. Do you not think the development of lay community implies that we must be open to vocations arising within the community, whether they be male or female? Did I understand you to say that women do not have a valid vocation to the priesthood today?

Oh dear no, I don't think women have a vocation to priesthood at all. I think they have a vocation to a ministry in the church which could be even more than priesthood, but the way all ministries are focussed on the male priest is extraordinary. Why should this one man have it all when there is such a diversity of ministries? Women should be ministering in equality with men and giving something which only women can give, so I think we will definitely see the clerical system break down gradually, and a more diverse ministerial community is already coming up in many cases, and will become the norm in the church.

Do you mean that within the diverse ministries which will develop, women should not celebrate the sacrament?

The sacramental is a problem; I think you have to leave these things to the Holy Spirit to work out. Although we look into the future, we cannot tell how these things are going to develop. It has to take place in the church as a whole, and our concept of sacrament has to grow also, so our theology will become more and more aware of the different needs, not only of women but of the whole problem of integrating other religious traditions into our life. We probably would not recognize the church in AD 3000.

There is a great sacramental tradition, the signs and symbols of the temple, and one of the things which is very interesting in the Indian Catholic church is the way that they are re-creating. They are developing different symbols. They make the shape of the church like a cave of the heart, like a cosmic egg. I find these new symbols very appealing, but then the problem is that as soon as you get into this world of sacred space and symbolism and so on you need priests. It is totally opposite from saying we should have lay communities where you don't have any symbols. To prevent quarrels you don't have any symbols but as soon as you have symbols you may have quarrels. Do you think the solution is to abandon symbolism and just have meditation? Or is it to have new symbols, relevant symbols which aren't oppressive but very liberating?

I think the community generates its own symbols. As you grow together you find a need to express your feelings and your own situation in gestures, in forms of different kinds, and you should create your own symbols and each shouldn't simply go off on its own. The symbolism should be related to the wider circle. This is just how the sacraments grew: each community discovers its own way of expressing its faith and its love, and creates its symbols.

In our community in Shantivanam there were three of us to begin with, and no structure behind us. I couldn't tell you how the liturgy has grown over twenty-five years. People have come and contributed this and that and the whole thing has grown to express the community's faith and understanding. That seems to me how a community should grow: you find your own symbols. You relate, of course, to people around you, it must not be too isolated, and so the church grows through new experiences of the mystery of faith. And finally in the new ways of expressing it you always have to keep a balance so that some people do not go off on their own with their own special symbols and lose touch with the rest. You have to keep the balance between the small community and the wider community, which is not always easy.

After coming back from India, I have found that the mystical body of Christ involves peoples of all religions.

Yes, I fully agree. Jesus didn't die for Jews or Christians, or anybody in particular; he died for all humanity. The grace of Christ in redemption extends to every human being, so the mystical body of Christ embraces all humanity from the first Adam to the last. The whole of humanity is an image of God, and we are all members of this common humanity ,and Jesus assumed humanity in himself and took it to God, so the whole of humanity constitutes in principle the mystical body of Christ.

In the light of other religions, do we have to rethink our position that Jesus is the only Son of God?

Yes. We have to take the biblical language always within its context. That Jesus experienced himself in a unique relationship to God as Father seems to me indisputable. In Matthew 11:27 we read that 'no one knows the Son but the Father; and no one knows the Father but the Son and those to whom the Son may choose to reveal him', so I believe Jesus experienced a unique relationship to God as Father, having this relationship of sonship and communicating with God in the Spirit. That, to me, is the unique Christian revelation. It is unique to Jesus and to his disciples and to the church. Other people have had other modes of experiencing God and they may have many gods, and many goddessess also, so each religion has its own symbols, its own language, its own mode of expressing the divine mystery. This is the Christian mystery, the expression of the Christian mystery in terms of the Trinity, Incarnation, Redemption, church; that to me is the Christian revelation, and it is unique; but it does not deny that the divine mystery is present in different modes, different expressions, different symbols, different language in different parts of the world.

What is your attitude towards reincarnation?

I always keep the distinction between the body, the soul, and the spirit. Reincarnation applies to the psyche, the soul; you are not your body, you are not your soul, you are this eternal spirit, which lives and acts in this body, in this soul. Your body in this form disintegrates in the end, and your psyche also disintegrates. Different people have different ideas about whether it goes on to another life or what happens to it, and I don't find any of them very interesting to be honest. I don't think it matters much what happens to the psyche – that's not you. Beyond your body, your psyche, your self, is your eternal spirit. When you pass from this life, this limited body and soul, to the eternal, you become one with the eternal Spirit and you bring with you your experience in the body and in the soul, but this body and this soul will not survive death. The body disintegrates, and the psyche (which depends on the physical body) also disintegrates. Jung's idea of the collective unconscious is that beneath our personal unconscious and our memories and so on we all relate with the past of humanity, so we all have a psychological inheritance. We have a physical inheritance which determines our physical form, and we have a psychological inheritance. Behind our personal being there is continuity with the past of humanity. People say they remember a past. They may be simply remembering various stages in the past of humanity through which we all come. This is not an explanation but it gives some indication of what may lie behind it. It's a rather opaque subject, reincarnation, and it doesn't appeal to me.

You spoke about the omnipresence of God. How do we see the integration of the polarities of good and evil?

This is a major problem. Humanity is not in the state in which it was originally intended to be. We have body, soul, and spirit, and at the beginning th/ e spirit was united with God and through the spirit the body and the soul could grow and mature. But when you don't follow the law of the spirit and keep yourself open to God, you fall into your psyche, into your ego, your separated self. To me, the Fall is from being one with God and humanity, into the individual separated self, the ego. All human problems arise from that evil separation. The word *diabolus* means to throw things apart, to disintegrate, and the devil is the power which disintegrates, which separates, which divides, and we live in this separated, divided, fallen world. Redemption is bringing back this divided humanity out of these separated egos, opening them up to the Spirit and reuniting humanity with God in Christ. Evil is egoism, a separated self, the essence of evil.

How can we today teach children to relate to the divine mystery in a world where they are out of touch with the natural world and technology has overtaken them?

I think this is a tremendous problem. Children grow up in a world where they are totally conditioned by this present world system, scientific and so on, and I think something has to happen before they can get out of it. It can be almost anything, sometimes sports: if you are skiing or something like that, you get a kind of ecstatic experience and you realize there is something beyond all this. Or it can be an accident – something happens, a physical accident, anything that breaks the routine, breaks through, opens you up. In *The Golden String* I described how when I was at school I was just an ordinary schoolboy, had no thoughts about religion, was very conventional, with no particular ideas at all, and when I was about seventeen I walked out one night at the playing fields in the evening and had an extraordinary experience, a sort of break-through. I saw there was a hawthorn bush with flowers, and it was like paradise to me. I thought I had never seen such a treat. Then I saw a lark rise up singing, and I thought how wonderful all this beauty around me was; it was a sudden revelation, and that can come to anybody. Anything that breaks through the routine suddenly opens you up to the other dimension; but something has to happen, I think, before the ordinary child growing up in this culture can get beyond it. It's so oppressive, so dominating, the television and everything, but something can happen to anybody to take them out of the whole thing.

The World Community
for Christian Meditation

Meditation in the tradition of the early Christian monks and as John Main passed it on has led to the formation of a world-wide community of meditators in over ninety countries. Weekly groups meet in many kinds of places and number over a thousand. An International Directory is maintained at the Community's London International Centre. A Guiding Board oversees the direction of the Community, a quarterly newsletter, the annual John Main Seminar, the School for Teachers, and the co-ordination of the Christian Meditation Centres around the world.

Medio Media

Founded in 1991, Medio Media is the publishing arm of the World Community for Christian Meditation. It is committed to the distribution of the works of John Main and many other writers in the field of contemplative spirituality and interfaith dialogue. Medio Media works in close association with the British publisher Arthur James. For a catalogue of books, audios, and videos contact Medio Media Ltd at the International Centre in London.

Christian Meditation Centres

International Centre
International Centre
The World Community for Christian Meditation
23 Kensington Square
London W8 5HN
Tel: 0171 937 4679
Fax: 0171 937 6790
e-mail: 106636.1512@compuserve.com

Australia
Christian Meditation Network
P.O. Box 6630
St Kilda Road
Melbourne, Vic. 3004
Tel: 03 989 4824
Fax: 03 525 4917

Christian Meditation Network
B.O. Box 323
Tuart Hill, WA 6060
Tel/Fax: 9 444 5810

Belgium
Christelijk Meditatie Centrum
Beiaardlaan 1
1850 Grimbergen
Tel: 02 269 5071

Brazil
Crista Meditacao Comunidade
CP 33266
CEP 22442-970
Rio de Janeiro RJ
Fax: 21 322 4171

Canada

Meditatio
P.O. Box 5523, Station NDG
Montreal, Quebec H4A 3P9
Tel: 514 766 0475
Fax: 514 937 8178

Centre de Méditation Chrétienne
Cap-Vie
367 Boulevard Ste-Rose
Tel: 514 625 0133

John Main Centre
470 Laurier Avenue, Apt 708
Ottawa, Ontario K1R 7W9
Tel: 613 236 9437
Fax: 613 236 2821

Christian Meditation Centre
10 Maple Street
Dartmouth, N. S. B2Y 2X3
Tel: 902 466 6691

India

Christian Meditation Centre
1/1429 Bilathikulam Road
Calicut
673006 Kerala
Tel: 495 60395

Ireland

Christian Meditation Centre
4 Eblana Avenue
Dun Laoghaire, Co. Dublin
Tel: 01 280 1505

Christian Meditation Centre
58 Meadow Grove
Blackrock, Cork
Tel: 021 357 249

Italy

Centro di Meditazione Cristiana
Abbazia di San Miniato al Monte
Via Delle Porte Sante 34
50125 Firenze
Tel/Fax: 055 2476302

New Zealand

Christian Meditation Centre
P.O. Box 35531
Auckland 1310

Philippines

5/f Chronicle Building Cor. Tektite Road
Meralco Avenue / Pasig
M. Manila
Tel: 02 633 3364
Fax: 02 631 3104

Singapore

Christian Meditation Centre
9 Mayfield Avenue
Singapore 438 023
Tel: 65 348 6790

Thailand

Christian Meditation Centre
51/1 Sedsiri Road
Bangkok 10400
Tel: 271 3295

United Kingdom

Christian Meditation Centre
29 Campden Hill Road
London W8 7DX
Tel/Fax: 0171 912 1371

Christian Meditation Centre
13 Langdale Road
Sale, Cheshire M33 4EW
Tel: 0161 976 2577

Christian Meditation Centre
Monastery of Christ the King
Bramley Road
London N14 4HE
Tel: 0181 449 6648
Fax: 0181 449 2338

Christian Meditation Centre
29 Mansion House Road
Glasgow
Scotland G41 3DN
Tel: 0141 649 4448

United States

John Main Institute
7315 Brookville Road
Chevy Chase, MD 20815
Tel: 301 652 8635

Christian Meditation Centre
1080 West Irving Park Road
Roselle, IL 60172
Tel/Fax: 630 351 2613

Christian Meditation Centre
322 East 94th Street No. 4B
New York, NY 10128
Tel: 212 831 5710

Christian Meditation Centre
2321 South Figueroa Way
Los Angeles, CA 90007-2501

Christian Meditation Centre
1619 Wight Street
Wall, NJ 07719
Tel: 908 681 6238
Fax: 908 280 5999

Christian Meditation Centre
2490 18th Avenue
Kingsburg, CA 93631
Tel: 209 897 3711

Hesed Community
3745 Elston Avenue
Oakland, CA 94602
Tel: 415 482 5573

Meditation on the Internet

WCCM.Archives
The WCCM, in collaboration with the Merton Research Institute
(Marshall University, USA), has archived a number of files: how to meditate; biographical information on John Main, Laurence Freeman, and
others; International Newsletters; catalogues of books, audiotapes, and
videotapes; the Rule of St Benedict and Benedictine oblates; the
International Calendar of events; John Main Seminars; New Testament
sources; and more. The Index of files and all individual files may be

retrieved by anonymous FTP or the WWW using the following URLs:

ftp://mbdu04.redc.marshall.edu/pub/merton/wccm/
http://www.marshall.edu/~stepp/vri/merton/wccm.html

The URLs for the Merton Archives are:

ftp://mbdu04.redc.marshall.edu/pub/merton/
http://www.marshall.edu/~stepp/vri/merton/merton.html

Merton-L is a forum for discourse on contemplative life. To subscribe, send e-mail to

listserv@wvnvm.wvnet.edu

containing the single line of text:

subscribe merton-l yourname

(substituting your real name for yourname, of course).

WCCM Forum

The WCCM.Forum is an outgrowth of the WCCM.Archives. Again, in collaboration with the Merton Research Institute, the expressed and sole purpose of the WCCM.Forum is to provide a place for substantive discussion on the daily practice of Christian Meditation as taught by John Main, the works of John Main and Laurence Freeman, and the work of the WCCM in general.

T6: WCCM, John Main, Laurence Freeman

In keeping with the expressed purpose of the WCCM.Forum as described above, posts about other types of meditation should not be posted to the T6 channel of Merton-L. (See the Merton-L faq for information about discussions on other channels.) Posts to T6 are moderated by the Merton-L owner(s) and are also monitored by T6 discussion leader, Gregory Ryan, who is the archivist of the WCCM electronic files. Questions or comments of a personal nature or suggestions concerning T6 may be submitted to Greg via e-mail:

gjryan@aol.com.

To subscribe to T6

To join the channel one must be a present member of Merton-L or, if not, subscribe to it. To subscribe to Merton-L, send e-mail to

listserv@wvnvm.wvnet.edu

containing the following single line of text:

subscribe merton-l yourname

(substituting your real full name for yourname, of course). Anyone who has subscribed to Merton-L may join the WCCM channel by sending e-mail to

listserv@wvnvm.wvnet.edu

(from your subscription address) containing the following single line of text:

set merton-l topics: +T6